# PATTERNS FOR
# TERRARIUMS
## and
# PLANTERS

*Wardell*
PUBLICATIONS

# ACKNOWLEDGEMENTS

## Pattern Designers

Randy Wardell, Judy Huffman,
Linda Holmes

## Project Fabrication

Linda Holmes, Ray Champeau

## Graphics and Layout

Steve Campbell, Linda Galloway

## Editor & Publisher

Randy Wardell

## Photography

Randy Wardell, Judy Huffman,
Jim Montgomery

## Plant Arrangements

Linda Holmes

**Terrariums & Planters (revised edition) is Copyright © 2003 by Wardell Publications Inc.**

Terrariums & Planters original edition was Published & Copyright© 1987 by R. A. Wardell

**Cataloguing in Publication Data**

Wardell, Randy A. (Randy Allan), 1954-

Patterns for Terrariums and Planters

ISBN 0-919985-02-5

1. Terrariums - Patterns   2. Plant Containers - Patterns

3. Glass craft - Patterns   4. Glass painting and Staining

I. Huffman, Judy,   II. Title

TT 298.W3  1984  748'.8  C84-098850-8

PUBLICATIONS INC

# CONTENTS

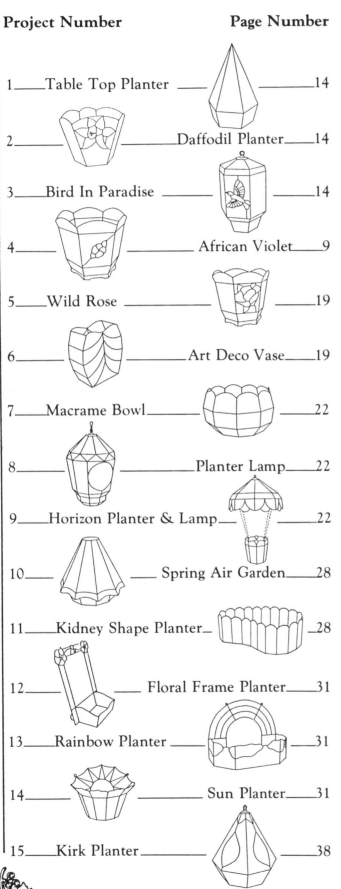
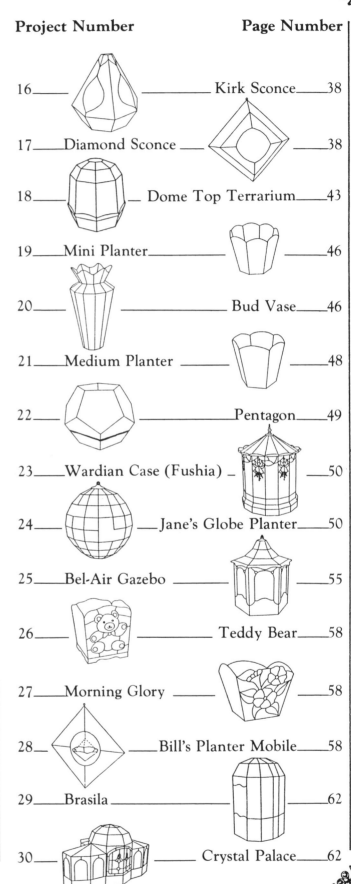

# Randy's Preface

Glass terrariums have always fascinated me. When planted and landscaped they remind me of elaborate Japanese gardens. Encased in glass, it is a mini-world that creates its own climate, complete with rain. A terrarium, in fact, was the first gift I gave my new found girlfriend, now my wife and esteemed co-author.

The terrarium we know today is directly descended from the Wardian case developed in the 1830's. Dr. Nathaniel Ward, an English surgeon, placed a cocoon, along with some soil, into a covered jar to observe a sphinx moth hatch from a chrysalis. Out of the soil sprouted a fern and for the next four years the fern prospered with no additional water or no influx of fresh air, until an accident occurred to the jar and the experiment came to an end.

Dr. Ward developed his discovery further and in 1842 published the results, complete with drawings. His small portable greenhouses came to be known as Wardian cases.

I used Dr. Ward's drawings as inspiration for the Wardian case project in this book. Except for a few changes to adapt the design to foil construction and the addition of the flowers, the design is true to his renderings.

The Wardian case, however, is only one of the 30 unique designs contained in this book. I have attempted to include something for everyone in terms of construction skill levels as well as different planter types and sizes.

Step by step photographs have been provided along with instructions to guide you through a typical project assembly. Some of the projects will require a good deal of experience in construction and will test even the most advanced crafter.

I feel this book is the most comprehensive collection of patterns and information for stained glass terrariums and planters available today and will provide you with many hours of challenge and satisfaction.
Keep those green thumbs up.

Randy

# Judy's Preface

Ah! To Enjoy the beauty of stained glass and plants!   Plants and their containers have always made a significant contribution to the decor of my home.

Friends sometimes refer to me as a "green thumber" but I feel my success is partly due to the variety of plants I choose. Through trial and error you will identify the plants which thrive best with your care and in your environment.

You will find in this book a section on plant suggestions which are some of the hardiest plant varieties for anyone who is not "Mr./Mrs. Green Thumber", plus a care section for your planted project.

I certainly hope this book entices you into enjoying plants more, by you the stained glass enthusiast, being able to create many beautiful containers for your plants and for gifts for family and friends.

Enjoy!

Judy

# HOW TO SECTION

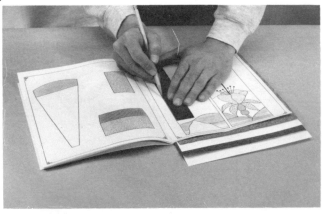

**1.** Trace patterns and make two copies, one on standard writing paper and one on heavy card (bristol board). Cut patterns from the card using scissors, the other copy will be your assembly guide.

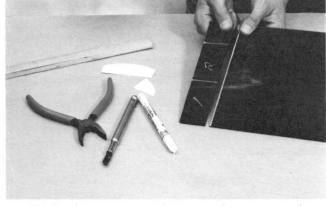

**2.** With a felt tip pen, carefully trace the pattern to the glass and cut out that piece. Check your glass piece to the pattern to be sure it is the same. If not exact, adjust your cutting to compensate on the next piece. To be accurate you must cut on the INSIDE of your traced line.

**3.** If the project you are building has a section with two or more pieces, they must be assembled as this time. The only way to do this with accuracy is to build a simple jig. (See photo.) Using the writing paper copy of the pattern you traced in Step 1, place it on your work table, face side up. You will need three or four straight edges (1" wide trim). Nail them along sides of the pattern so the outside line of the section to be assembled is just showing along the straight edge.

**4.** Place all your glass pieces into the jig as your pattern shows. If your pieces do not fit in so that they lie flat, it is because you have cut them too large. You should check the jig to be sure it is nailed in the correct spot, but usually some glass pieces will need a bit of grinding (or grozzing).

**5.** Once all of the pieces fit correctly, clean each piece of glass, then copper foil it. Be sure to press the foil to the edge of the glass using a wood lathkin.

**6.** Place the foiled glass pieces into the jig and solder them together. Since the outside is facing up, put a finish bead on it. Remove the section from the jig, turn it over and solder the inside. Repeat for each multi-piece section in your project.

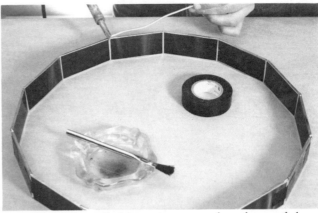

**7.** It is now time to start the assembly of your project. In most cases you should assemble the row of glass which is at the bottom of your project first. Lay these pieces good side up on the work bench side by side in their proper order. Using black plastic electrical tape, tape the sections together (see photo). Use a straight edge to keep the glass pieces even.

**8.** Carefully pull this section around to shape of the bottom piece of glass. Tack solder each piece together at the top joint only.

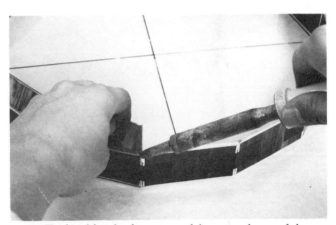

**9.** Place the bottom glass piece on your bench and position your assembly on top. Tack solder from the inside, one corner joint which meets the base. Next, tack solder the seam directly opposite. Repeat this tack soldering alternating from side to side until all joints are fastened.

**10.** Tack solder the first piece of the second row of glass to the base. Place the second piece on and tack it to the base. Gently pull together piece one and two so the seam meets evenly and tack solder together. Add piece three and so on around the project, tacking one to the other as you go. When the complete row is tacked together, solder the seams inside and out.

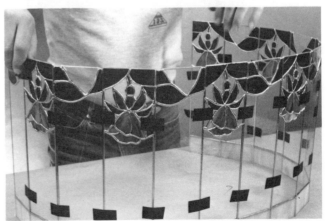

**11.** Lay main body panels on your work bench good side up in their proper order. Tape sections together with black plastic electrical tape. Use a straight edge to keep the glass panels even (see photo).

**12.** Carefully, pull this section around to the shape of your base. Tape together.

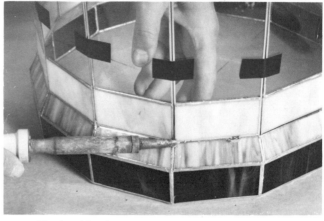

**13.** Carefully, lift up your main body section and position it on top of your base assembly so all seams line up.

**14.** Tack solder from the outside one joint which meets the base. Next, solder the seam directly opposite. Repeat this tack soldering, alternating from side to side, until all are fastened. Tack solder all joints at the top.

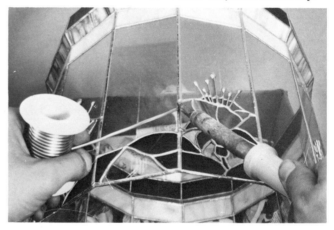

**15.** It is important at this time to solder a reinforcing wire (copper or brass, 18 gauge) around the top of your project.

**16.** Gently, lay your project into your soldering box (a cardboard box with crumpled newspapers inside). Solder all inside seams and bead solder all the outside seams.

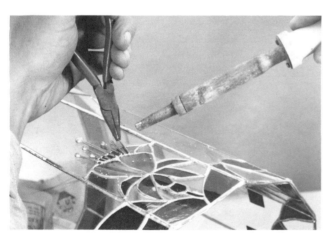

**17.** After all soldering is complete, clean your project with a glass cleaner. Solder or attach any overlay details your project requires at this time.

**18.** Time now to assemble the lid of our project. Lay all your glass pieces good side up on your work bench side by side in their proper order. Using black plastic electrical tape, tape the sections together.

**19.** Carefully raise this section up into a cone shape, keeping the large diameter end on the bench. Bring the two ends together and tape.

**20.** Depending on your project, solder a vase cap or glass piece into place. Leaving your project on your work bench, flat solder all outside seams (black tape should be left on). See photo.

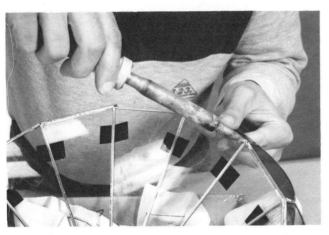

**21.** Turn your project upsidedown and place in the soldering box. Attach the trim row of glass to the lid by using the same techniques as described in Step 10.

**22.** When all pieces have been added, complete soldering the inside and put a finish bead on the outside.

**23.** Clean your project with a glass cleaner and patina if desired.

**24.** To seal the base to prevent leakage, we use a clear silicone sealant (bathtub caulking). Let dry overnight. Your project is now ready for planting (See Section on *How to Plant your Terrarium*).

# A GARDEN IN GLASS...

A simple combination of a glass container, soil, rocks, charcoal, air water and plants makes a terrarium the easiest and most beautiful way to grow and display plants in your home. You can decorate your home and observe at first-hand the miracle of plants thriving in a protected environment.

Your plants will keep green and glossy in the moist air inside your terrarium with little watering. Healthy, clean-leafed, moisture flecked plants under a glass enclosure you have created, will command the attention and the praise of others.

Now, it happens that some plants will not tolerate that much protection. Unlike the terrarium, the glass planter has no controlled climate, the gardener has to provide the water, humidity and any other vital necessities.

Glass containers offer mobility and versatility, from serving as a centerpiece at a dinner party to decorating a coffee table or window, all applications will attract the indoor gardener.

If you do not happen to be a greenthumber or the planter is to be located in an area with little or no sunlight, a super alternative is to use silk or dried plants. These are readily available from many florists and you can make a pleasing arrangement for very little cost and virtually no maintenance.

# SUGGESTIONS OF PLANTS YOU CAN USE FOR YOUR TERRARIUM:

- Choose small but healthy-looking plants.
- Select miniature varieties as seedlings whenever possible.
- A number of different kinds of plants will give an interesting variety of foliage shapes and colours. Use three, four, or five specimens for each terrarium depending on size of both plants and terrariums, leaving room for future growth.

- Aluminum Plant (Pilea Cadierei)
- Baby's Tears (Helxine Soleirolii)
- Gold Dust Plant (Dracaena Godseffiana)
- Nerve Plant (Fittonia)
- Emerald Ripple (Peperomia Caperata)
- Variegated Peperomia (Peperomia Obtusifolia Variegat)
- Ribbon Plant (Dracaena Sanderiana)
- Parlor Palm (seedling) )Chamaedorea Elegans)
- Button Fern (Pellaea Rotundifolia)
- Asparagus Fern (Asparagus Plumosus)
- Strawberry Geranium (Saxifraga Sarmentosa)

# PLANTER POTS:

All of the above suggestions plus many, many, more can be planted in your planter pot.
**Please Note:** African Violets thrive best in an open container. Cacti and Succulents are Not recommended for closed terrariums.

To enhance your terrarium and planter pots (i.e. miniature garden styles) be your own landscape artist. Those tiny shells you picked up at the beach, a special stone or two, and small pieces of driftwood all work. It takes just a few carefully chosen found objects like these to add to the beauty you have already created with your own stained glass craftsmanship.

# CARE OF YOUR PLANTED TERRARIUM:

Watch your terrarium closely during the first few weeks after planting. The environment (heat, light, temperature etc.) in which you place it will determine the frequency of its watering requirements and rate of plant growth.

If too much condensation (moisture) forms on the lid, open the terrarium for a few hours. It is a good idea to open your glass terrarium occasionally; (monthly) to allow air to circulate briefly and to check the soil for adequate moisture. *Again, Do Not Overwater.*

Remove any dropped foliage and thin out rapidly growing plants when foliage becomes too thick. Six months after planting feed your plants with a house plant fertilizer (formula 25-15-20).

# HOW TO PLANT YOUR TERRARIUM

**Step 1**
(a) Place gravel (coarse aquarium gravel is excellent for this purpose) into bottom of terrarium to a depth of approximately ½ inch.

(b) Add ¼ inch layer of charcoal

(c) Pour soil on top of the gravel and charcoal to a depth of no more than 2/3 of the container. Landscape your terrarium soil keeping in mind the plants you will be using and decorative found objects you will possibly incorporate. We recommend you use a commercially prepared, indoor plant soil.

**Step 2**
Scoop holes, and set in the plants as planned. Give each plant growing room. Look at your arrangement from all sides and make sure the plant's shape fits. Firm soil about the roots. Remove any dirt from plants' leaves with a small brush (artist's) or spray lightly with plant sprayer.

**Step 3**
Water sparingly. ***Never Overwater!*** The soil should be moist, but not soaked or saturated. A terrarium has a self-regulating environment which recycles moisture and air to support plant growth.

**Step 4**
Put the glass lid on your terrarium. Let your terrarium sit in a shady area for a day so your newly transplanted plants can rest. This is not absolutely necessary but it will help the plants adjust to their new home. Thereafter, keep your terrarium in good light but ***never in direct sunlight.***

## Table Top Planter | SKILL LEVEL- Beginner | Project 1

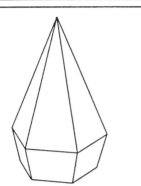

### SPECIFICATIONS

| | |
|---|---|
| # Pieces— | 10 |
| Overall Height— | 10" |
| Diameter— | 6½" |

Project Patterns on page 15

### MATERIALS

— ½ sq. ft.— Alternating Beige & Green Opal

— 1 sq. ft.— Clear

**Special Instruction—** To make into a hanging planter, solder support wire from pot, up sides and form a loop at the top.

## Daffodil Planter | SKILL LEVEL— Int. | Project 2

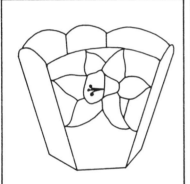

### SPECIFICATIONS

| | |
|---|---|
| # Pieces— | 49 |
| Overall Height— | 6½" |
| Width— | 7" |
| Diameter— | 8½" |

Project Patterns on pages 15 & 16
Fits a 5" Plastic Flower Pot

### MATERIALS

— 1½ sq. ft.— Lt. Blue Opal

— sm. piece— Solid Yellow

— ½ sq. ft.— Med. Blue Opal

— ½ sq. ft.— Whispy Yellow

— sm. piece— Lt. Yellow

**Special Instruction—**
Use Pattern 'A' on Pg. 15 for bottom.
Use 12 Gauge wire for stamen overlays.

## Bird In Paradise | SKILL LEVEL- Int./Adv. | Project 3

### SPECIFICATIONS

| | |
|---|---|
| # Pieces— | 54 |
| Height— | 13" |

Project Patterns on pages 15, 17, 18.
Use Patterns "A" "B" from pg. 15 for bottom section.

### MATERIALS

— 1¾ sq. ft.— Clear

— ¾ sq. ft.— Cath. Brown

— ½ sq. ft.— Cath. Amber

— sm. piece— Op. Dk. Orange/Red

— sm. piece— Op. Lt. Orange

— sm. piece— Op. Orange

— sm. piece— Brown

Vase Cap— 2½"

**Special Instruction—**
Use a 7½" rod and tube hinge set for door.
Use wire overlays on bird wings.

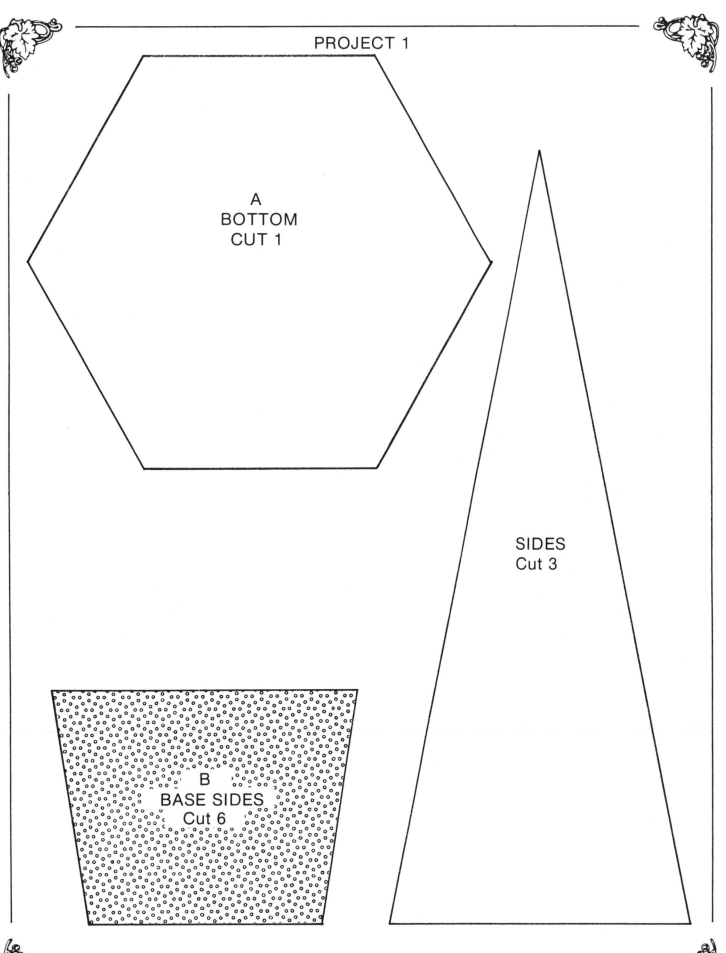

A
BOTTOM
CUT 1

SIDES
Cut 3

B
BASE SIDES
Cut 6

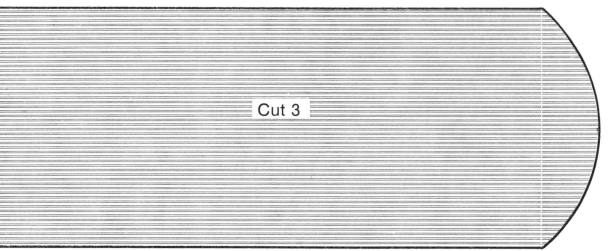

Cut 3

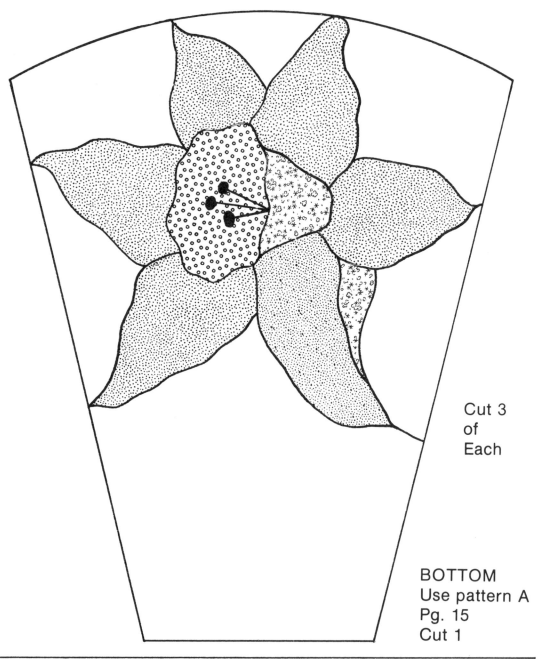

Cut 3
of
Each

BOTTOM
Use pattern A
Pg. 15
Cut 1

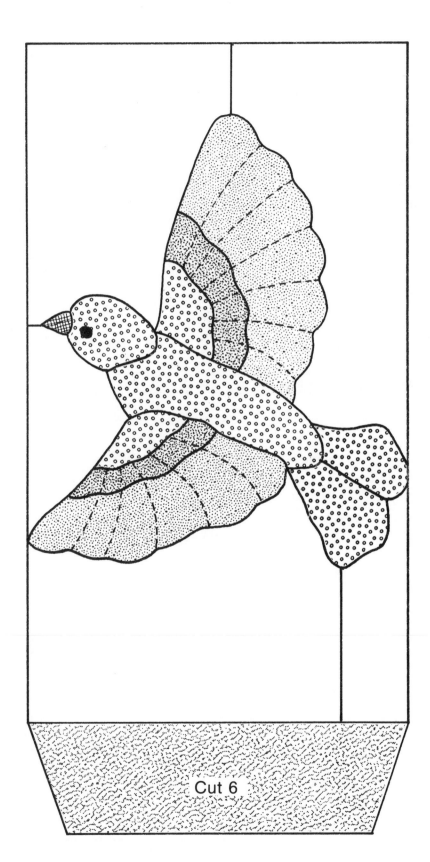

Cut and assemble
1 Bird panel.

Cut 4 plain panels
using outside
line only.

Cut 6

BOTTOM
Use pattern A page 15.

FIRST ROW OF BASE
Use pattern B page 15.

Cut 6

Cut 6

DOOR PANEL
Cut 1 of each.

## African Violet · SKILL LEVEL- Beg./Int. · Project 4

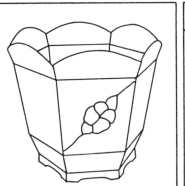

### SPECIFICATIONS

| | |
|---|---:|
| # Pieces— | 46 |
| Height— | 6" |
| Width— | 6½" |

Project Patterns on page 20.
Fits a 5" Flower Pot

### MATERIALS

- — 1¼ sq. ft.— white opal
- — 1/3 sq. ft— Mauve Cath.
- — ¼ sq. ft— Lt. Mauve Opal
- — sm. piece— Dk. Mauve Opal
- — sm. piece— Dk. Green Opal

**Special Instruction—**
The glass pedestal (feet) are optional.

---

## Wild Rose · SKILL LEVEL- Beg./Int. · Project 5

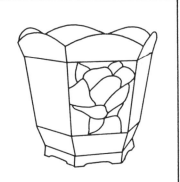

### SPECIFICATIONS

| | |
|---|---:|
| # Pieces— | 70 |
| Height— | 6" |
| Width— | 6½" |

Project Patterns on pages 20.
Fits a 5" Flower Pot

### MATERIALS

- — 1¼ sq. ft.—Lt. Green Opal
- — 1/3 sq. ft.— Cath. Red
- — ¼ sq. ft.— Med. Green Opal
- — 1/3 sq. ft.— Pink Opal
- — 1/8 sq. ft— Dk. Green Cathedral

**Special Instruction—**
The glass pedestal (feet) are optional.

---

## Art Deco Vase · SKILL LEVEL- Beg./Int. · Project 6

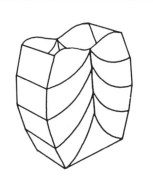

### SPECIFICATIONS

| | |
|---|---:|
| # Pieces— | 27 |
| Height— | 6" |
| Width— | 5¾" |
| Depth— | 2½" |

Project Patterns on pg. 21.

### MATERIALS

- — 1/3 sq. ft.— Orange Opal
- — ¼ sq. ft.—
- — ¼ sq. ft.—     To
- — ¼ sq. ft.—
- — ¼ sq. ft.—     Red

**Special Instruction—**
Use any colour progression format from Lt. to Dk. starting at the top.

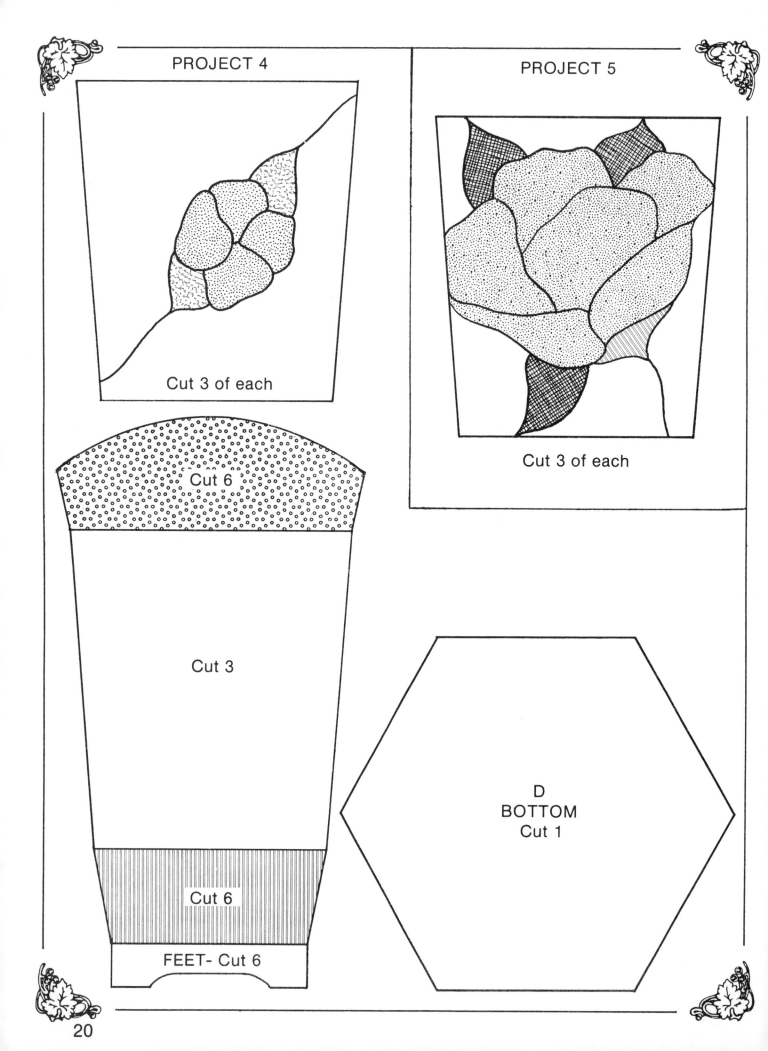

PROJECT 4

Cut 3 of each

PROJECT 5

Cut 3 of each

Cut 6

Cut 3

Cut 6

FEET- Cut 6

D
BOTTOM
Cut 1

BOTTOM
Cut 1

Cut 2 of each color
Total of 8

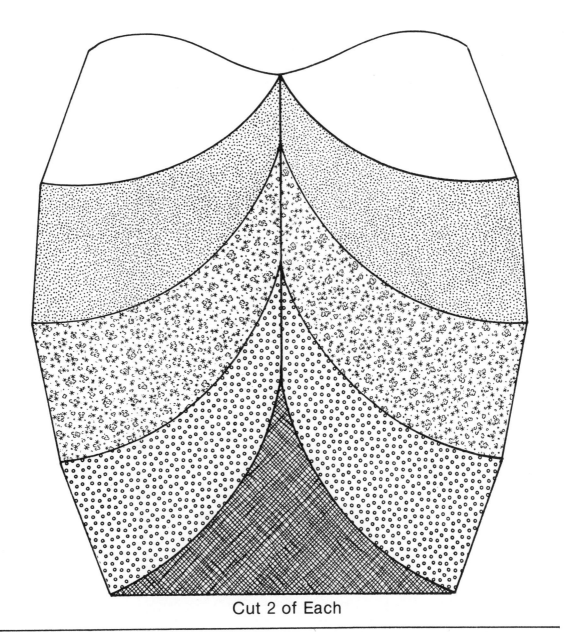

Cut 2 of Each

| Macrame Bowl | SKILL LEVEL- Beginner | Project 7 |
| --- | --- | --- |

## SPECIFICATIONS

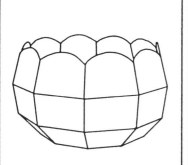

| # Pieces— | 31 |
| Height— | 5" |
| Width— | 8" |

Project Patterns on page 23.

## MATERIALS

☐ — 2¼ sq. ft. Total—
Lt. & Dk. Mauve Opal
Alternating

**Special Instruction—**

This pot works well in a macrame hanger.

---

| Planter Lamp | SKILL LEVEL- Int./Adv. | Project 8 |
| --- | --- | --- |

## SPECIFICATIONS

| # Pieces— | 75 |
| Height— | 20" |
| Diameter— | 13" |

Project Patterns on pages 23, 24
& 25.

## MATERIALS

☐ — 3¼ sq. ft.— Clear

▦ — 3¼ sq. ft.— Beige
(includes Row 1) pg. 23

▤ — ½ sq. ft.— Med. Brown
Cath.

Row 2— 2/3 sq. ft— Brown Opal

Vase Cap— 3½"

**Special Instruction—**

Use Row 1 & Row 2 & Bottom of Project 7.
Use a full spectrum incandescent grow bulb.

---

| Horizon Planter & Lamp | SKILL LEVEL— Int. | Project 9 |
| --- | --- | --- |

## SPECIFICATIONS

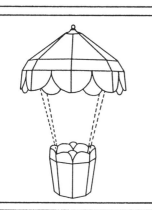

| # Pieces— | 61 |
| Lampshade Height— | 9" |
| Diameter— | 14½" |
| Pot- Height- | 6½" |
| Diameter- | 6" |

Project Patterns on pages 26 & 27

Fits a 5" Flower Pot

## MATERIALS

☐ — 4¼ sq. ft.— Whispy White
Opal

▥ — 1¼ sq. ft.— Whispy Aqua

▨ — 1 sq. ft.— Cath. Aqua

Brass U Hook- 4

Med. Link
Brass Chain— 4 pcs.-13" Long

**Special Instruction—**

Solder 3" of chain to inside of every other seam on the pot. Solder a
U hook to every other inside seam of the lamp to fasten chain.

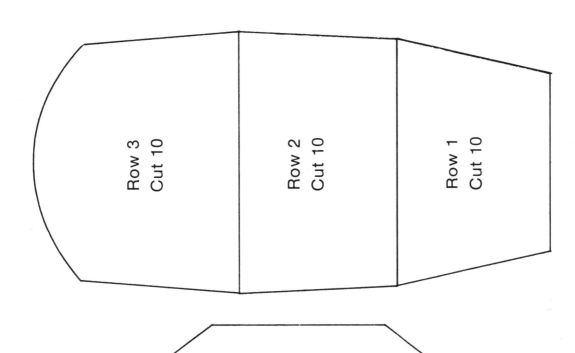

Row 3
Cut 10

Row 2
Cut 10

Row 1
Cut 10

BOTTOM
Cut 1

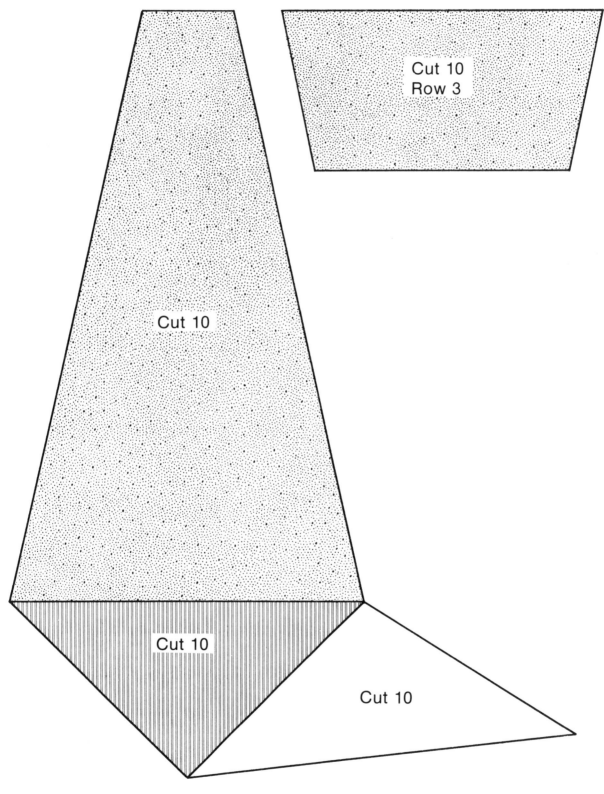

Cut 10
Row 3

Cut 10

Cut 10

Cut 10

Cut 2 up
2 down

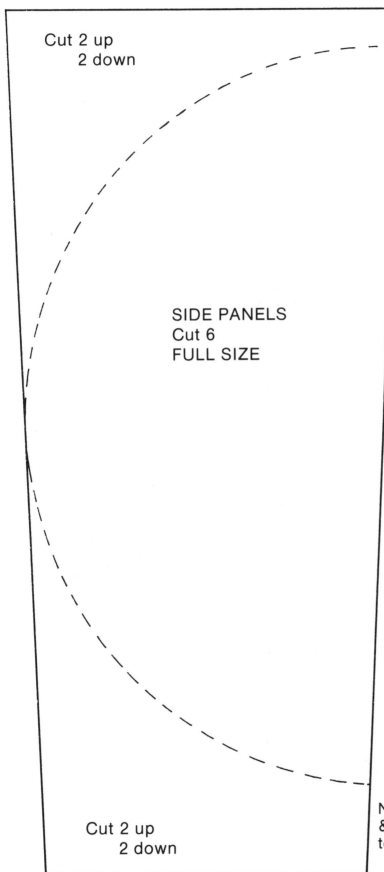

SIDE PANELS
Cut 6
FULL SIZE

Cut 2 up
2 down

NOTE: Use Bottom Pattern and Row 1
& Row 2 Patterns for lower section of
terrarium from page 23- project 7.

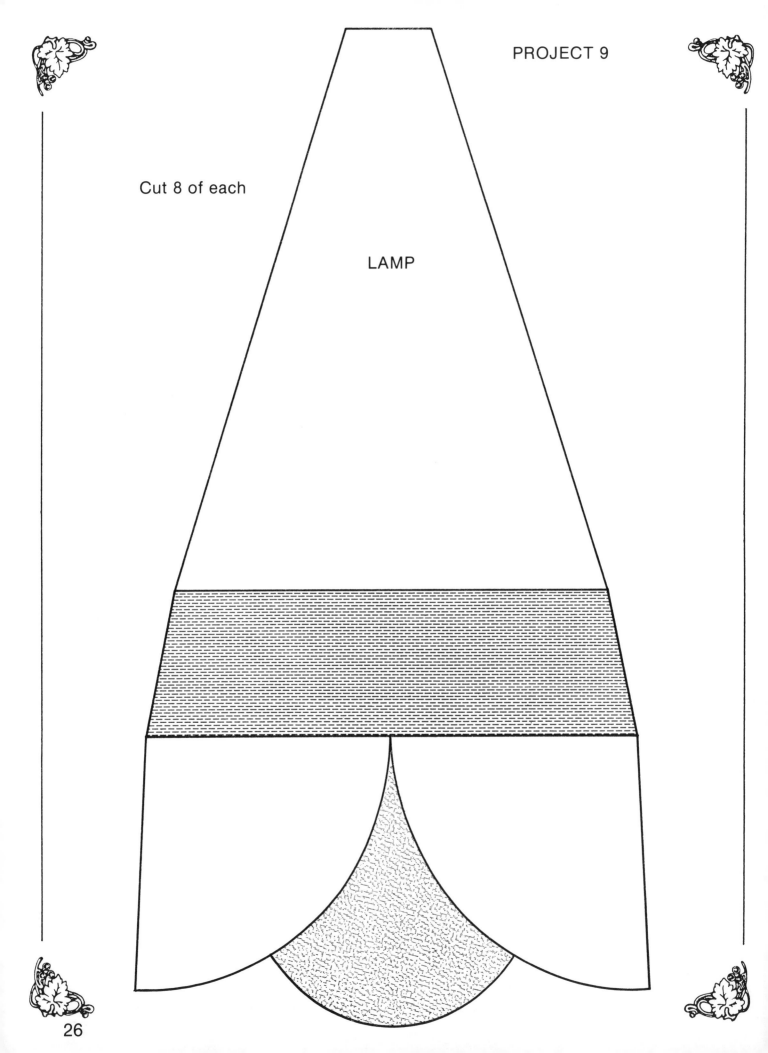

Cut 8 of each

LAMP

Cut 4

Cut 4 Up
Cut 4 Down

PLANTER POT
Cut 8

Bottom
Cut 1

## Spring Air Garden | SKILL LEVEL- Beginner | Project 10

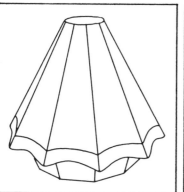

### SPECIFICATIONS

| | |
|---|---|
| # Pieces— | 32 |
| Overall Height— | 9" |
| Diameter— | 8" |

Project Patterns on pages 28, 29.

### MATERIALS

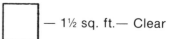

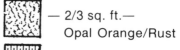

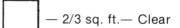

— 1½ sq. ft.— Clear

— 2/3 sq. ft.— Opal Orange/Rust

— ½ sq. ft.— Cath. Amber

### Special Instruction—
The cone shape top sits on the base and is not fastened.

## Kidney Shape Planter | SKILL LEVEL- Beginner | Project 11

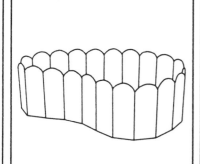

### SPECIFICATIONS

| | |
|---|---|
| # Pieces— | 22 |
| Length— | 11" |
| Height— | 3½" |

Project Patterns on page 30.

### MATERIALS

— 2/3 sq. ft.— Clear

— 1 sq. ft.- Opal Blue/Green

### Special Instruction—
Makes a great cactus container, but remember to seal with silicone or line with plastic before planting.

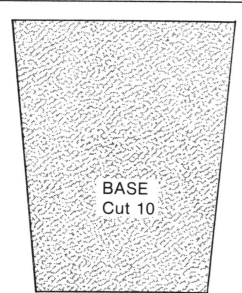

PROJECT 10

BASE
Cut 10

TOP
Cut 1

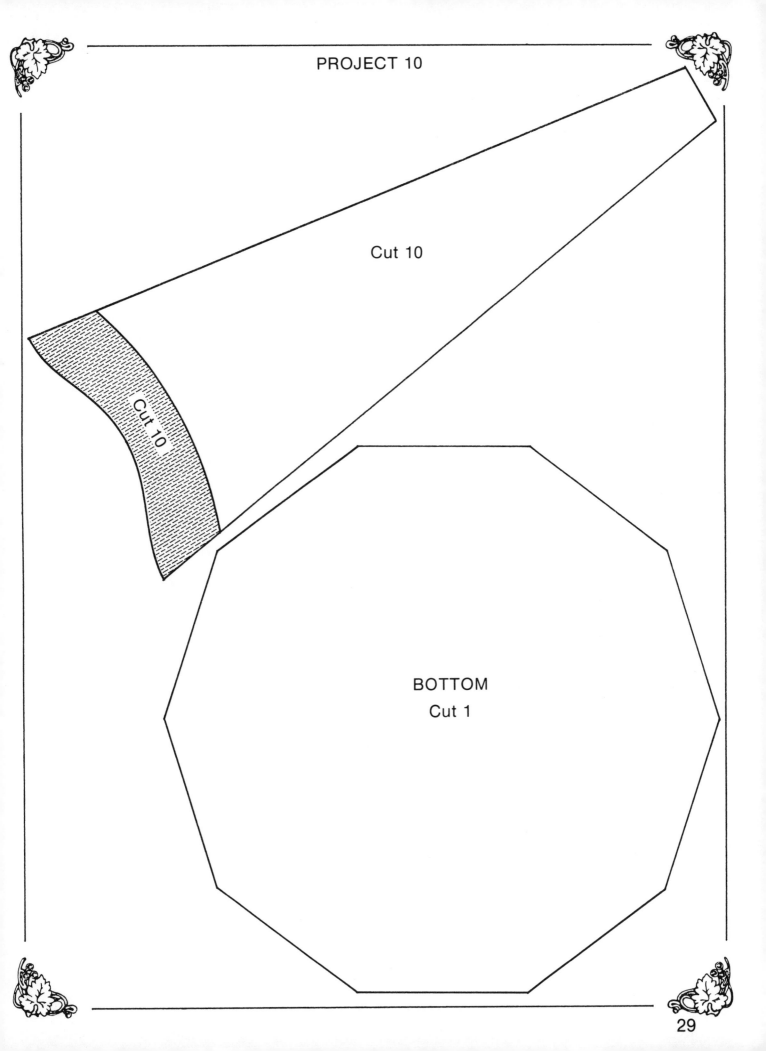

Cut 10

Cut 10

BOTTOM
Cut 1

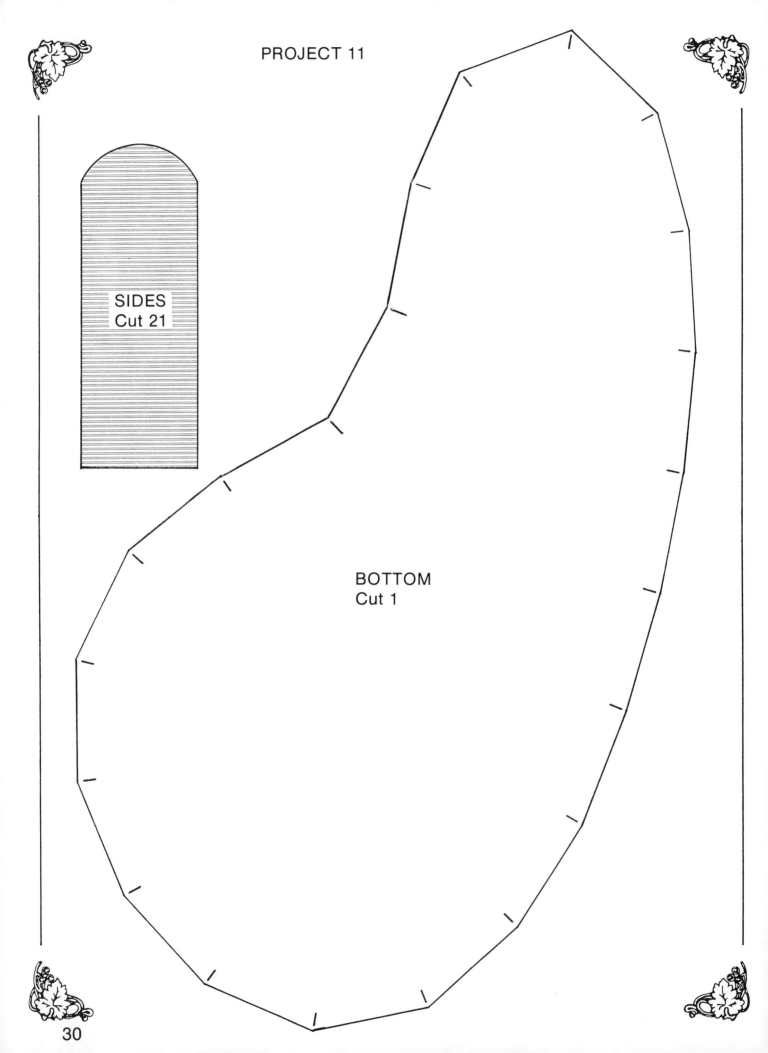

SIDES
Cut 21

BOTTOM
Cut 1

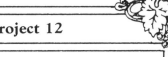

| Floral Frame Planter | SKILL LEVEL- Beg./Int. | Project 12 |
| --- | --- | --- |

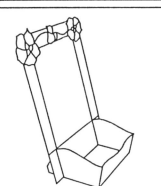

## SPECIFICATIONS

| | |
| --- | --- |
| # Pieces— | 37 |
| Height— | 10" |
| Width— | 7" |
| Front Pot— | 5 X 3½" |
| Picture Size— | 5 X 7" |

Project Patterns on page 32 & 33

## MATERIALS

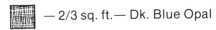 — 1/3 sq. ft.— Clear

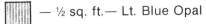 — ½ sq. ft.— Lt. Blue Opal

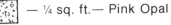 — 2/3 sq. ft.— Dk. Blue Opal

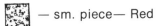 — ¼ sq. ft.— Pink Opal

— sm. piece— Red

— sm. piece— Dk. Green Opal

**Special Instruction—**
The leaves and flowers are overlays. Solder photo corner brackets onto back of frame to secure picture.

| Rainbow Planter | SKILL LEVEL- Beg./Int. | Project 13 |
| --- | --- | --- |

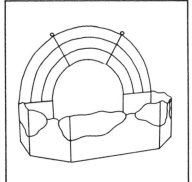

## SPECIFICATIONS

| | |
| --- | --- |
| # Pieces— | 26 |
| Length— | 10" |
| Overall Height— | 8" |

Project Patterns on pages 34, 35, 36.

## MATERIALS

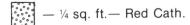 — 1 sq. ft.— Med. Blue Opal

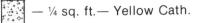 — ¼ sq. ft.— Red Cath.

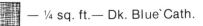 — ¼ sq. ft.— Yellow Cath.

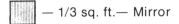 — ¼ sq. ft.— Dk. Blue Cath.

— 1/3 sq. ft.— Mirror

— ½ sq. ft.— White Opal

**Special Instruction—**
Solder wire loops on back seams of rainbow for hanging.

| Sun Planter | SKILL LEVEL- Beg./Int. | Project 14 |
| --- | --- | --- |

## SPECIFICATIONS

| | |
| --- | --- |
| # Pieces— | 28 |
| Length— | 9" |
| Overall Height— | 8" |

Project Patterns on page 36 & 37.

## MATERIALS

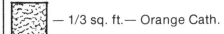 — ¾ sq. ft.— Beige Opal

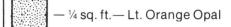 — 1/3 sq. ft.— Orange Cath.

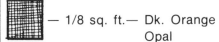 — ¼ sq. ft.— Lt. Orange Opal

 — 1/8 sq. ft.— Dk. Orange Opal

— sm. piece— Solid Orange Opal

**Special Instruction—**
Solder wire loops on back seams of sun rays for hanging.

31

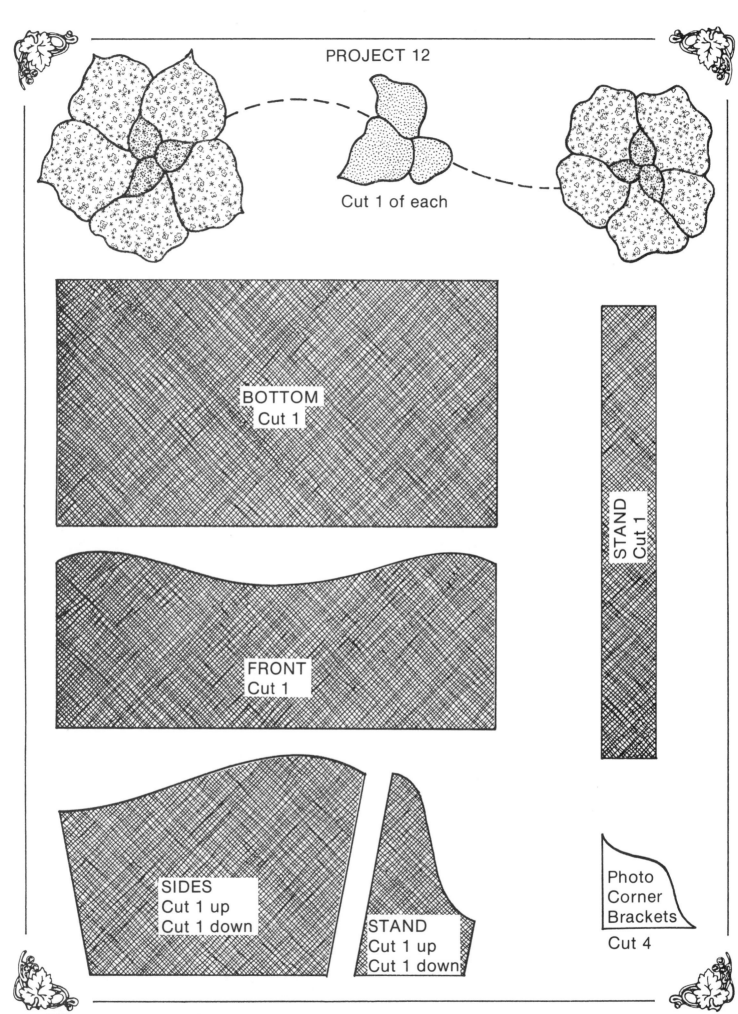

PROJECT 12

Cut 1 of each

BOTTOM
Cut 1

STAND
Cut 1

FRONT
Cut 1

SIDES
Cut 1 up
Cut 1 down

STAND
Cut 1 up
Cut 1 down

Photo
Corner
Brackets
Cut 4

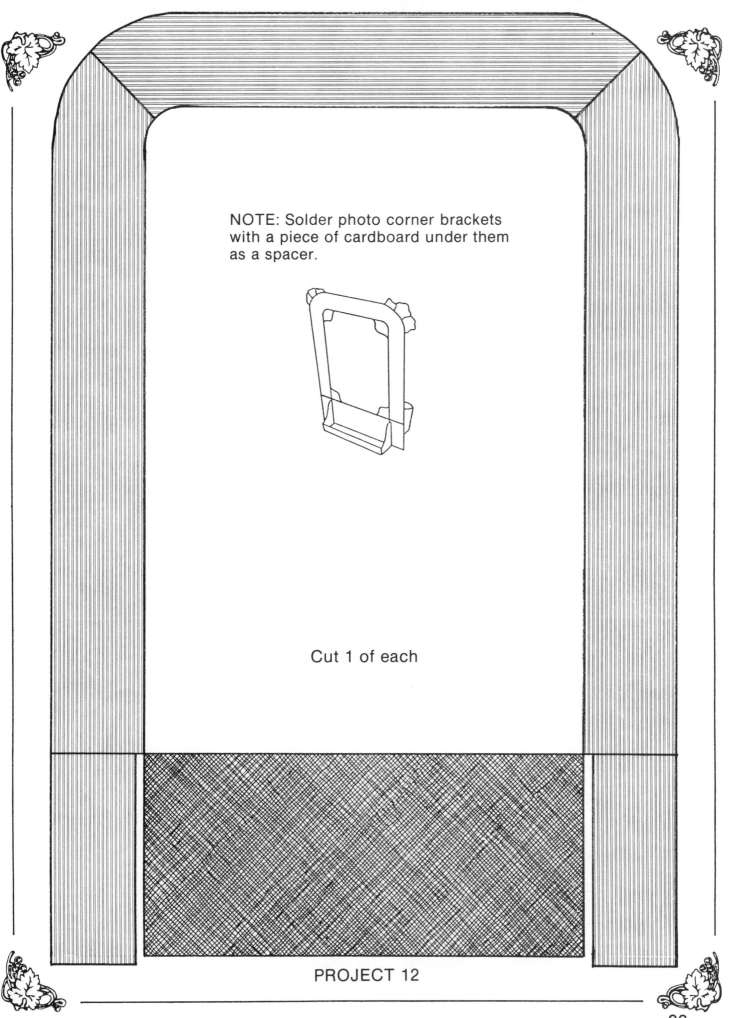

NOTE: Solder photo corner brackets with a piece of cardboard under them as a spacer.

Cut 1 of each

PROJECT 12

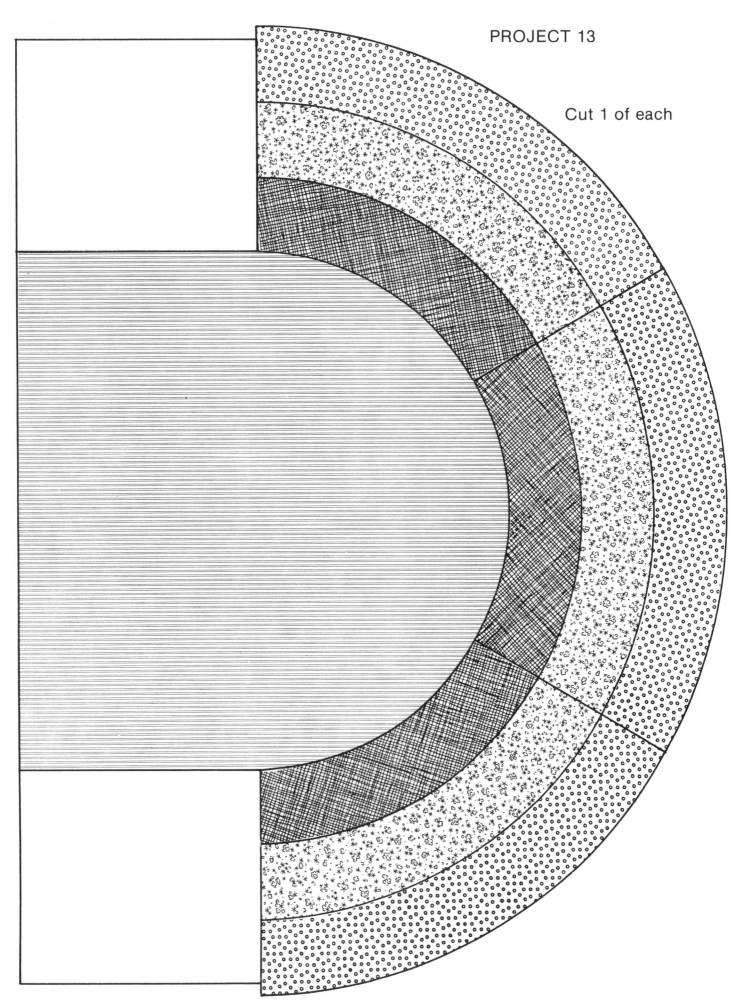

PROJECT 13

Cut 1 of each

34

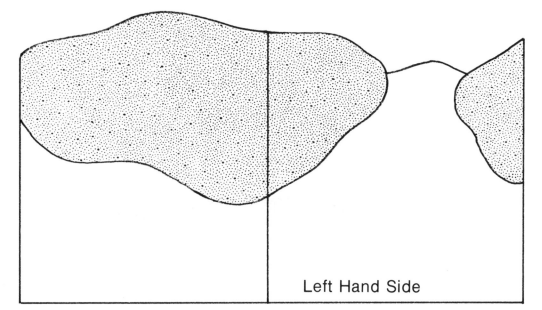

Left Hand Side

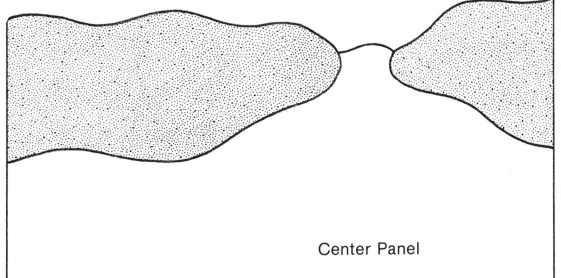

Cut 1
of each

Center Panel

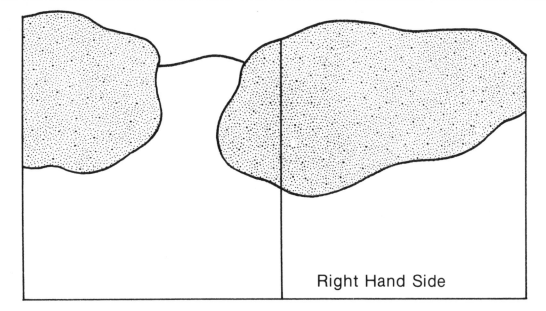

Right Hand Side

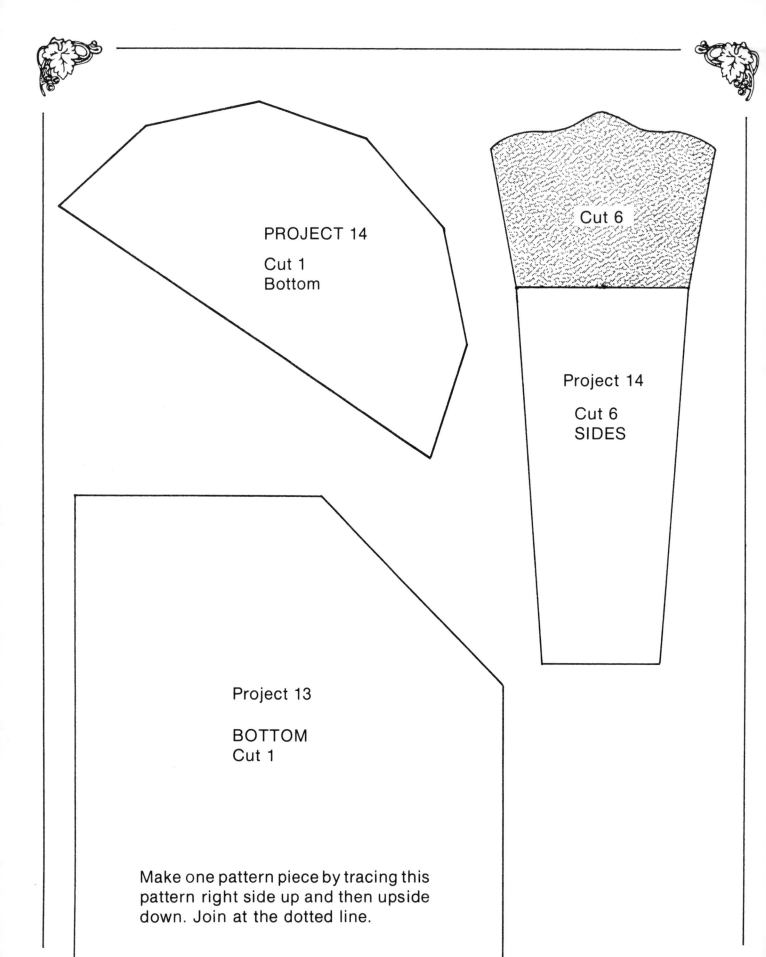

PROJECT 14

Cut 1
Bottom

Cut 6

Project 14

Cut 6
SIDES

Project 13

BOTTOM
Cut 1

Make one pattern piece by tracing this
pattern right side up and then upside
down. Join at the dotted line.

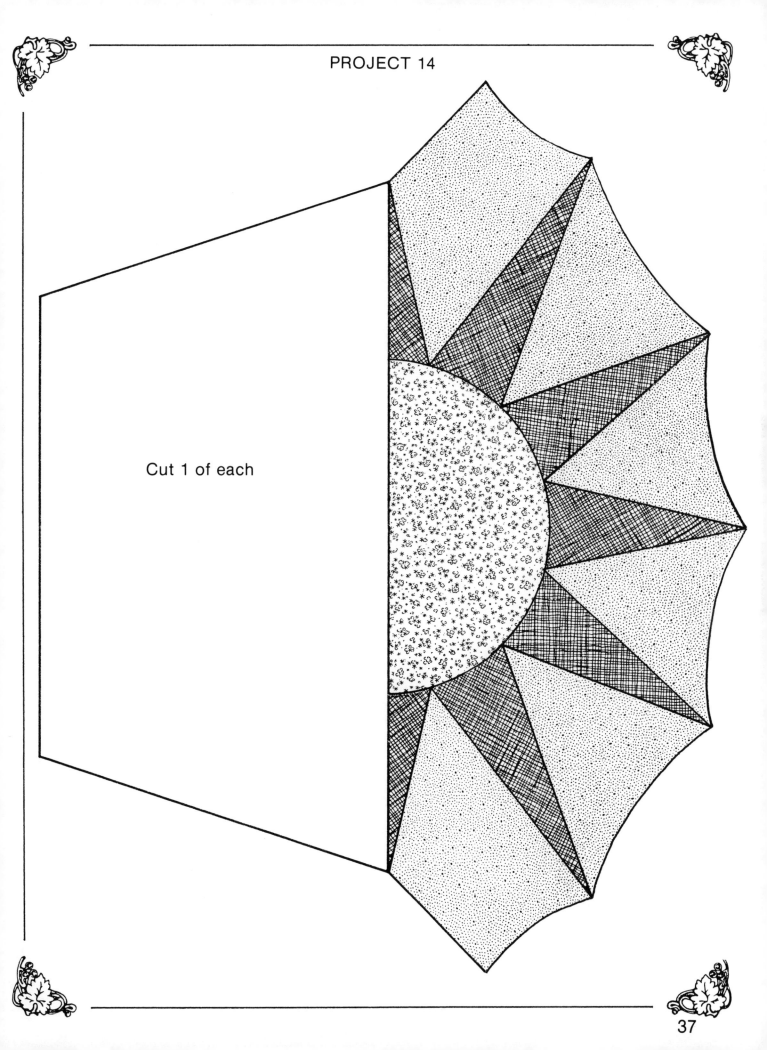

Cut 1 of each

## Kirk Planter     SKILL LEVEL- Beg./Int.    Project 15

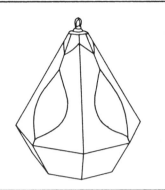

### SPECIFICATIONS

| | |
|---|---|
| # Pieces— | 25 |
| Height— | 12" |
| Width— | 11" |

Project Patterns on pages
39 & 40

### MATERIALS

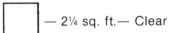

— 2¼ sq. ft. — Clear

— 1¾ sq. ft. — Med. Blue Opal

— ¼ sq. ft.— Blue Cath.

Vase Cap— 1½"

**Special Instruction—**

Can be a hanging planter or table top planter.

---

## Kirk Sconce    SKILL LEVEL— Int.    Project 16

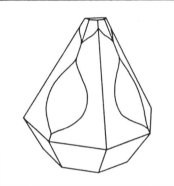

### SPECIFICATIONS

| | |
|---|---|
| # Pieces— | 14 |
| Height— | 12" |
| Width— | 11" |
| Depth— | 6" |

Project Patterns on pages
39, 40 & 41.

### MATERIALS

— 1 1/3 sq. ft.— Clear

— 2/3 sq. ft.— Lt. Green Opal

— sm. piece— Green Cath.

Back— 12"x 12"- Green Mirror

**Special Instruction—**
Use Patterns A, B & C from Pg. 39 (Project 15). Solder a heavy (12) gauge wire up side seams to make a loop for hanging.

---

## Diamond Sconce    SKILL LEVEL- Beginner    Project 17

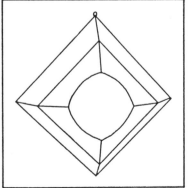

### SPECIFICATIONS

| | |
|---|---|
| # Pieces— | 9 |
| Height— | 10" |
| Width— | 10" |
| Depth— | 4" |

Project Patterns on page 42.

### MATERIALS

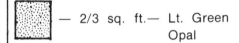

— 1¾ sq. ft.— Clear

Back piece- 10"x 10"— Bronze Mirror

**Special Instruction—**
Cut a 10"x 10" square for back. Solder a heavy (12) gauge wire up side seams to make a loop for hanging.

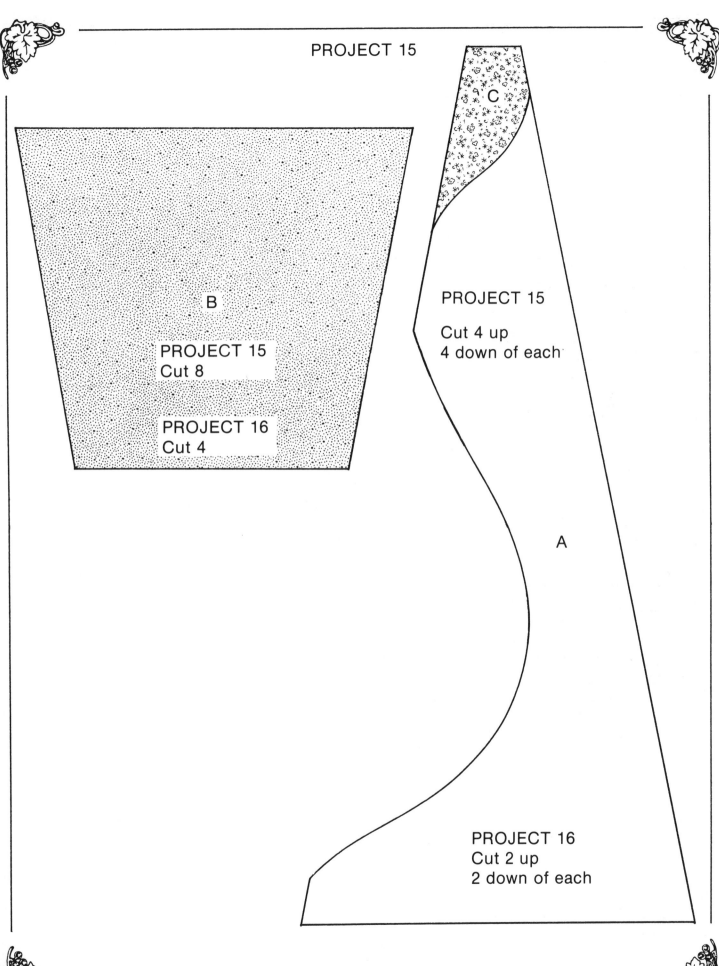

C

PROJECT 15

Cut 4 up
4 down of each

B

PROJECT 15
Cut 8

PROJECT 16
Cut 4

A

PROJECT 16
Cut 2 up
2 down of each

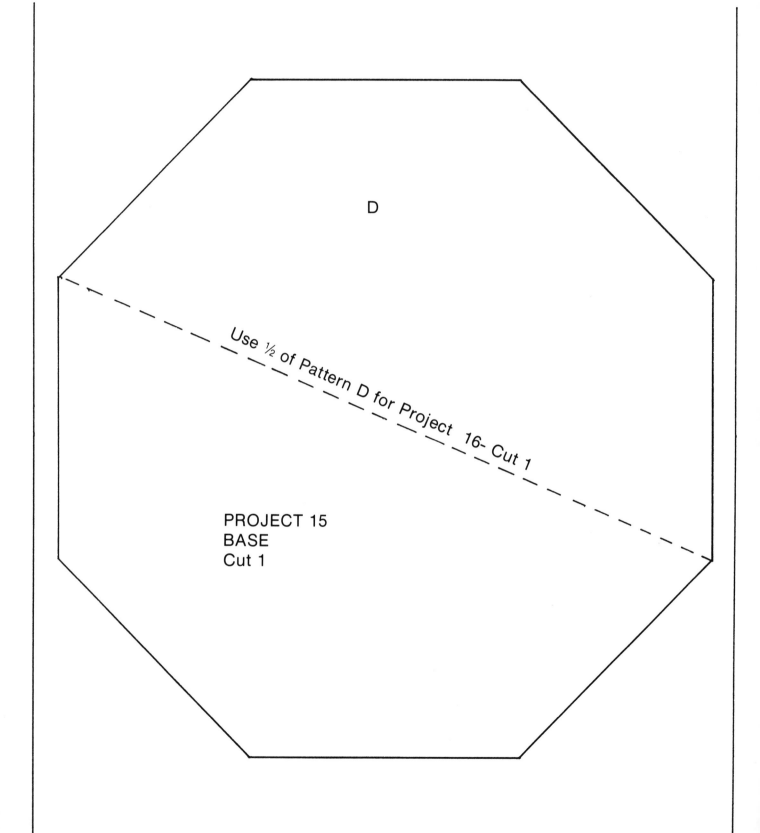

D

Use ½ of Pattern D for Project 16- Cut 1

PROJECT 15
BASE
Cut 1

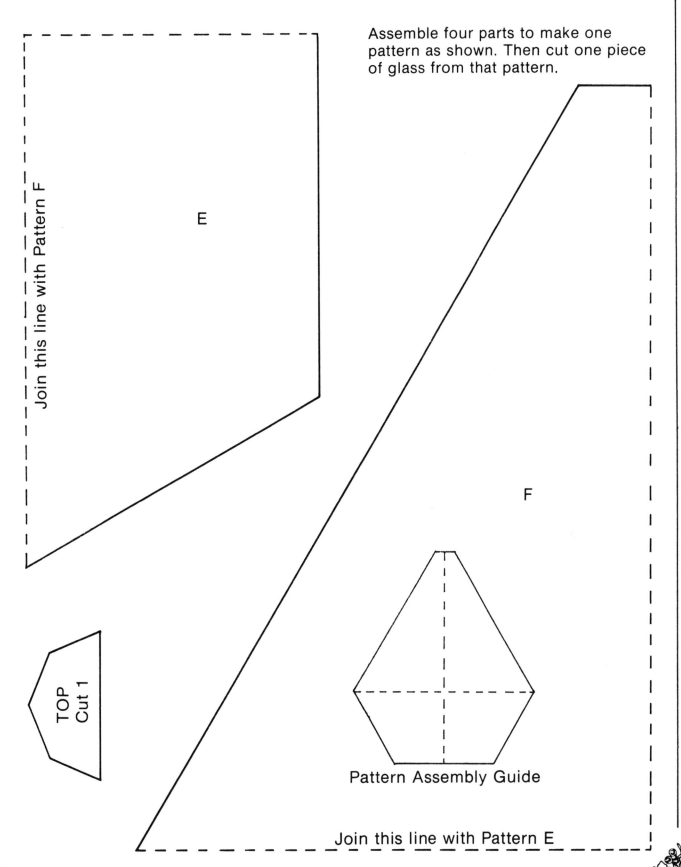

Assemble four parts to make one pattern as shown. Then cut one piece of glass from that pattern.

Join this line with Pattern F

E

F

TOP
Cut 1

Pattern Assembly Guide

Join this line with Pattern E

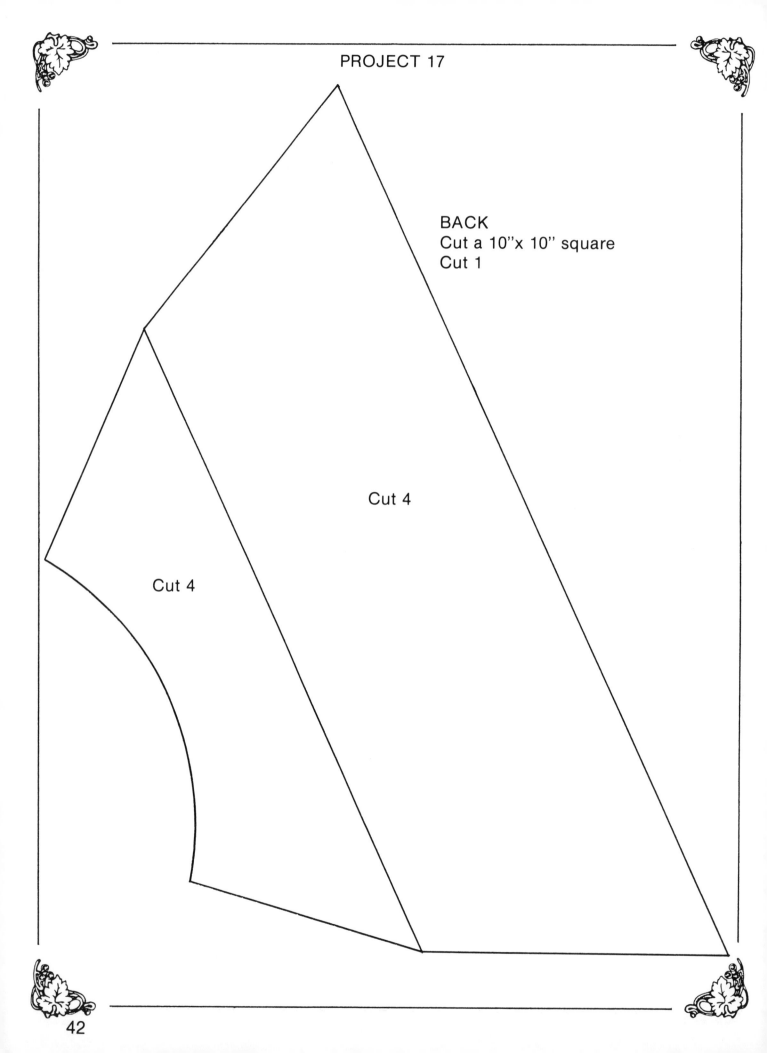

BACK
Cut a 10"x 10" square
Cut 1

Cut 4

Cut 4

| Dome Top Terrarium | SKILL LEVEL— Int. | Project 18 |
|---|---|---|

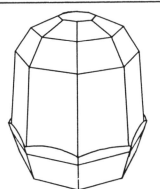

## SPECIFICATIONS

| # Pieces— | 42 |
|---|---|
| Height— | 13" |
| Diameter— | 12" |

Project Patterns on pages
43, 44, 45.

## MATERIALS

— 7 sq. ft.— Clear

— 2 sq. ft.— Brown Opal

— ½ sq. ft.— Beige Opal

**Special Instruction—**
This dome lid is designed to fit just inside top row on base.

PROJECT 18

Cut 8

Cut 8
BASE

ROW 1
Cut 8

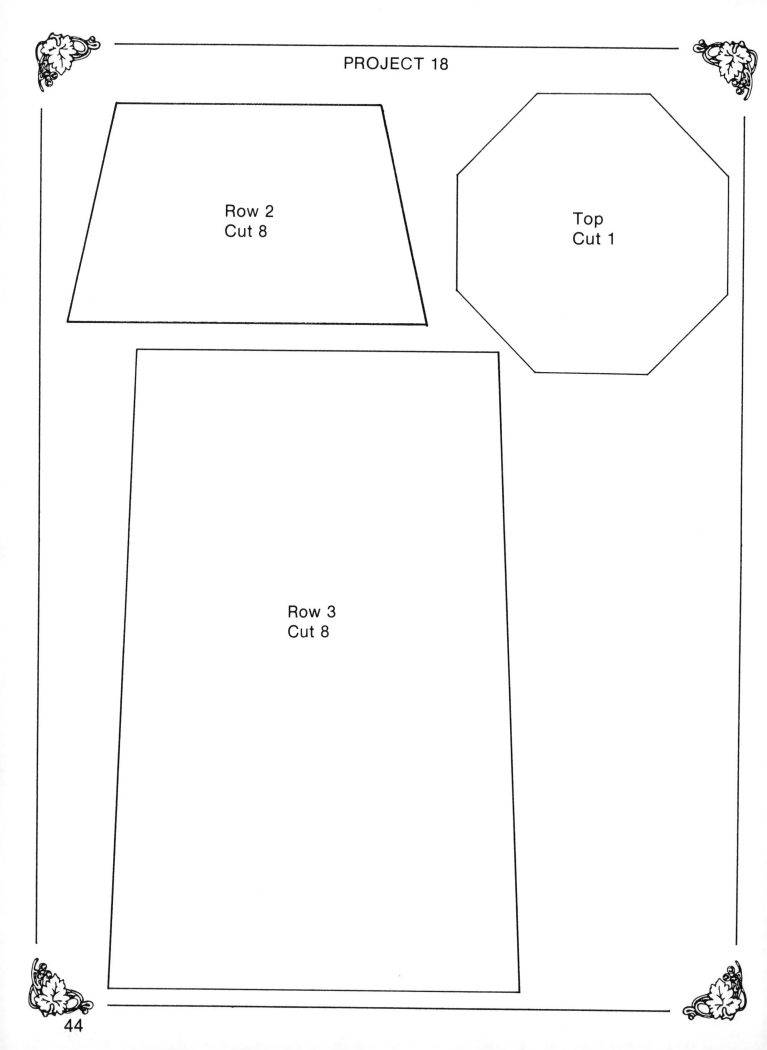

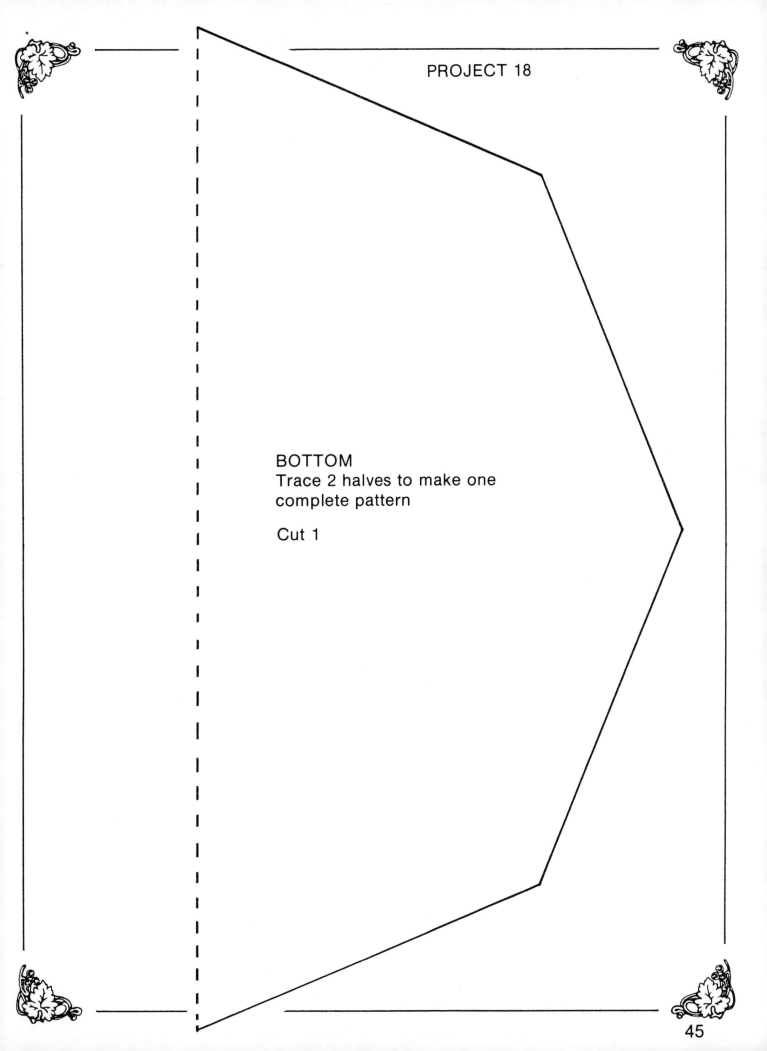

BOTTOM
Trace 2 halves to make one
complete pattern

Cut 1

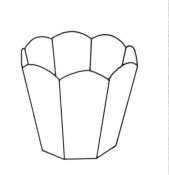

## SPECIFICATIONS

| | |
|---|---|
| # Pieces— | 9 |
| Height— | 4½" |
| Width— | 5" |

Project Patterns on pages 46 & 47

Fits a 4" Flower Pot

## MATERIALS

— ¾ sq. ft.— Alternating Pink/White Opal

**Special Instruction—**

A super beginner project.

---

**Bud Vase** | **SKILL LEVEL—** Int. | **Project 20**

## SPECIFICATIONS

| | |
|---|---|
| # Pieces— | 37 |
| Height— | 9½" |
| Width— | 5" |

Project Patterns on page 47.

## MATERIALS

— 1¾ sq. ft.— Whispy Orange/Clear

**Special Instruction—**
Must solder inside completely before adding each row.
This vase is best for artificial/dried flowers.

---

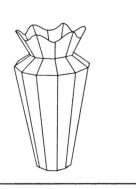

SIDES
Cut 8

PROJECT 19

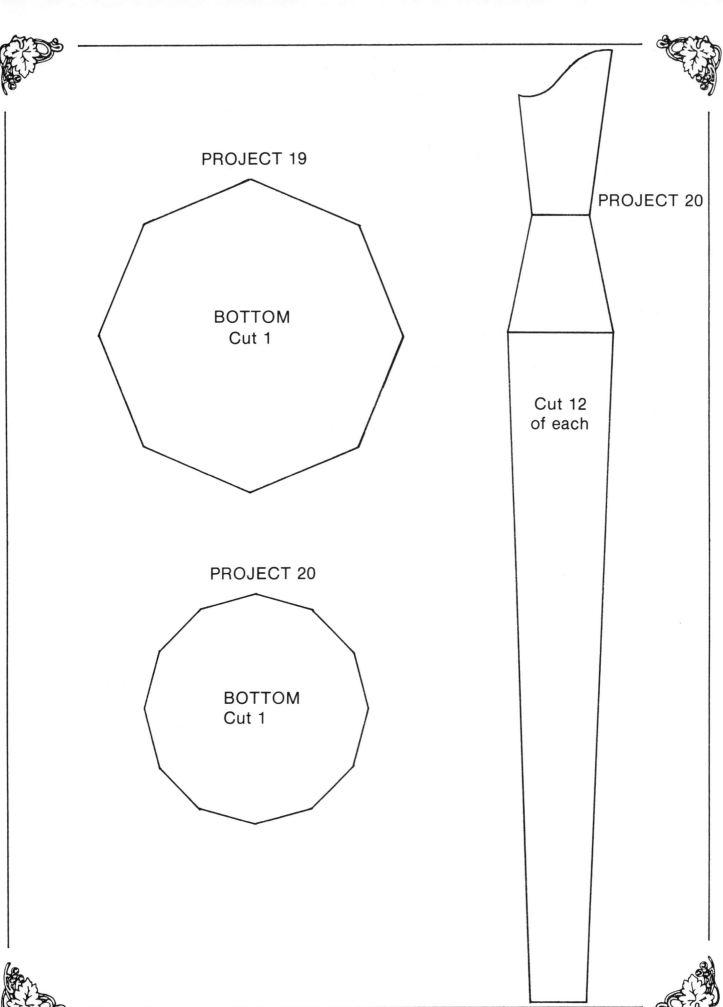

PROJECT 19

BOTTOM
Cut 1

PROJECT 20

BOTTOM
Cut 1

PROJECT 20

Cut 12
of each

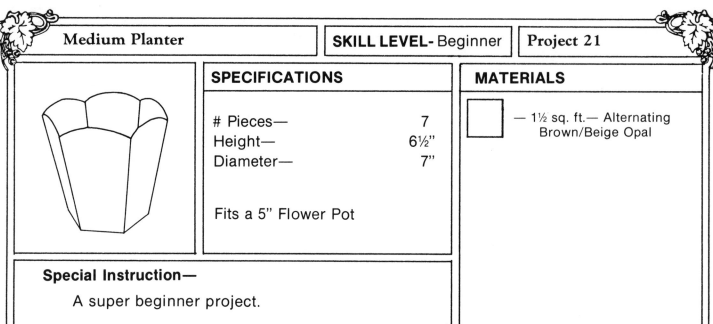

## SPECIFICATIONS

| | |
|---|---|
| # Pieces— | 7 |
| Height— | 6½" |
| Diameter— | 7" |

Fits a 5" Flower Pot

## MATERIALS

— 1½ sq. ft.— Alternating Brown/Beige Opal

**Special Instruction—**

A super beginner project.

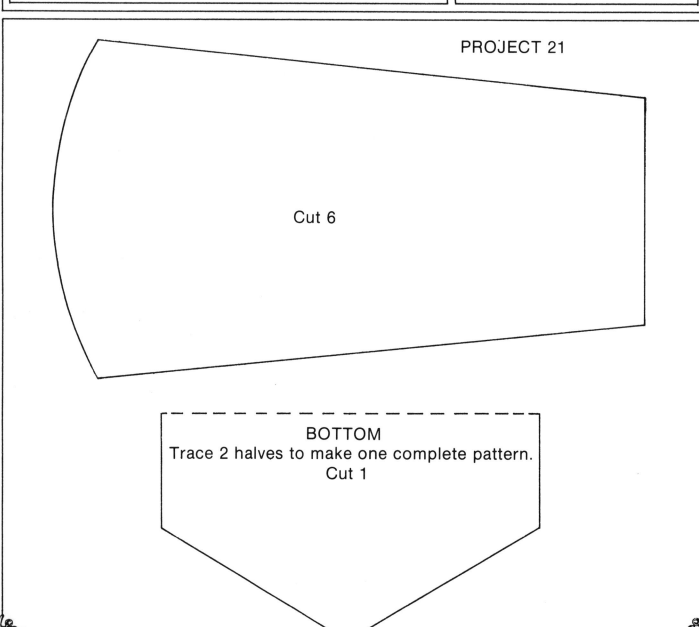

PROJECT 21

Cut 6

BOTTOM
Trace 2 halves to make one complete pattern.
Cut 1

| Pentagon | SKILL LEVEL- Beginner | Project 22 |
|---|---|---|

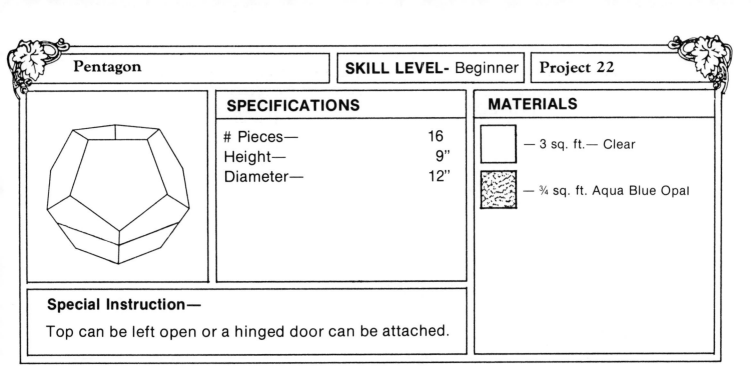

### SPECIFICATIONS

| # Pieces— | 16 |
|---|---|
| Height— | 9" |
| Diameter— | 12" |

### MATERIALS

— 3 sq. ft.— Clear

— ¾ sq. ft. Aqua Blue Opal

**Special Instruction—**

Top can be left open or a hinged door can be attached.

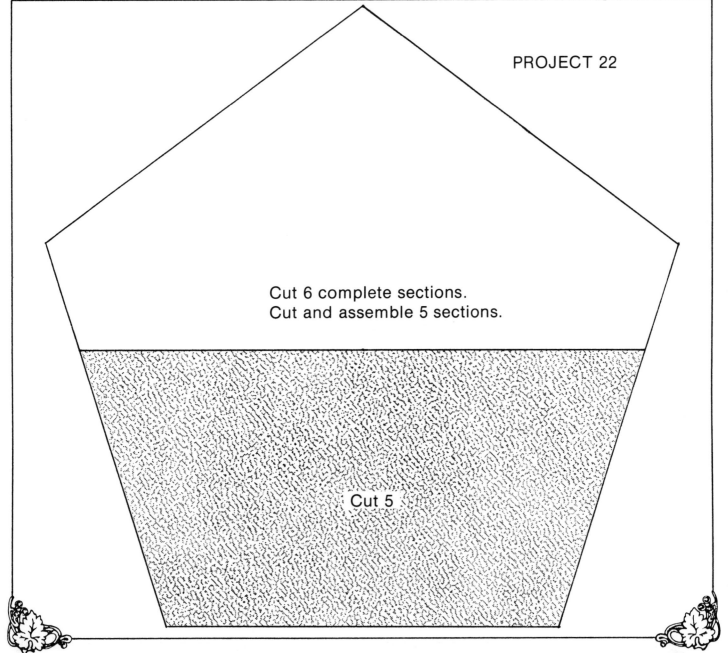

PROJECT 22

Cut 6 complete sections.
Cut and assemble 5 sections.

Cut 5

| Wardian Case (Fushia) | SKILL LEVEL— Adv. | Project 23 |

## SPECIFICATIONS

| | |
|---|---|
| # Pieces— | 253 |
| Height— | 18" |
| Diameter— | 14½" |

Project Patterns on pages
50, 51, 52 & 53.

## MATERIALS

— 8 sq. ft.— Clear
— 1½ sq. ft.— Dk. Green Opal
— ½ sq. ft.— Med. Green Opal
— 1 sq. ft.— Pink Opal
— 2/3 sq. ft.— Lt. Green Opal
— ¾ sq. ft— Dk. Green Cath.
- sm. piece— Dk. Green Cath.
- ½ sq. ft— Pink Cath.
Vase Cap— 2"

## Special Instruction—
Use wire overlays for flower stamens.
Solder a heavy gauge wire around top edge of planter.

| Jane's Globe Planter | SKILL LEVEL— Adv. | Project 24 |

## SPECIFICATIONS

| | |
|---|---|
| # Pieces— | 122 |
| Height— | 26" |
| Diameter— | 18" |

Project Patterns on pages
53 & 54

## MATERIALS

— 8 sq. ft.— Clear

— 2 sq. ft.— Dk. Green Opal

Vase Cap— 4½" top
— 5" bottom (opt.)

## Special Instruction—
Leave open spaces of glass at several points around the globe.
Solder a wire from the bottom to top following an inside seam along every fourth seam.

PROJECT 23

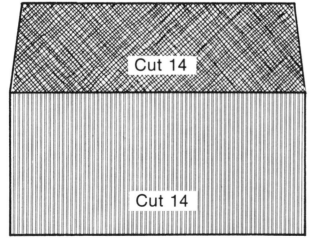

Cut 14

Cut 14

Cut 14

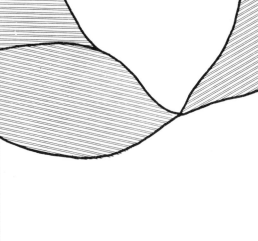
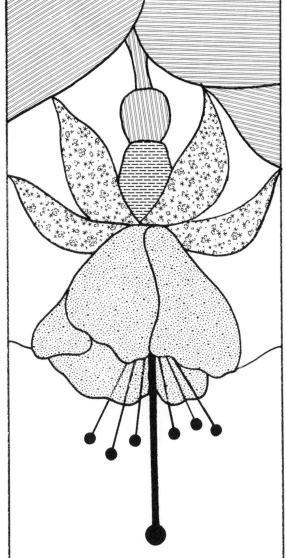

Cut 7 of each

Cut 7 of each

BOTTOM
Cut 1

NOTE: Trace two patterns right side up
and two patterns upside down. Cut out
and tape together to make one pattern
piece.

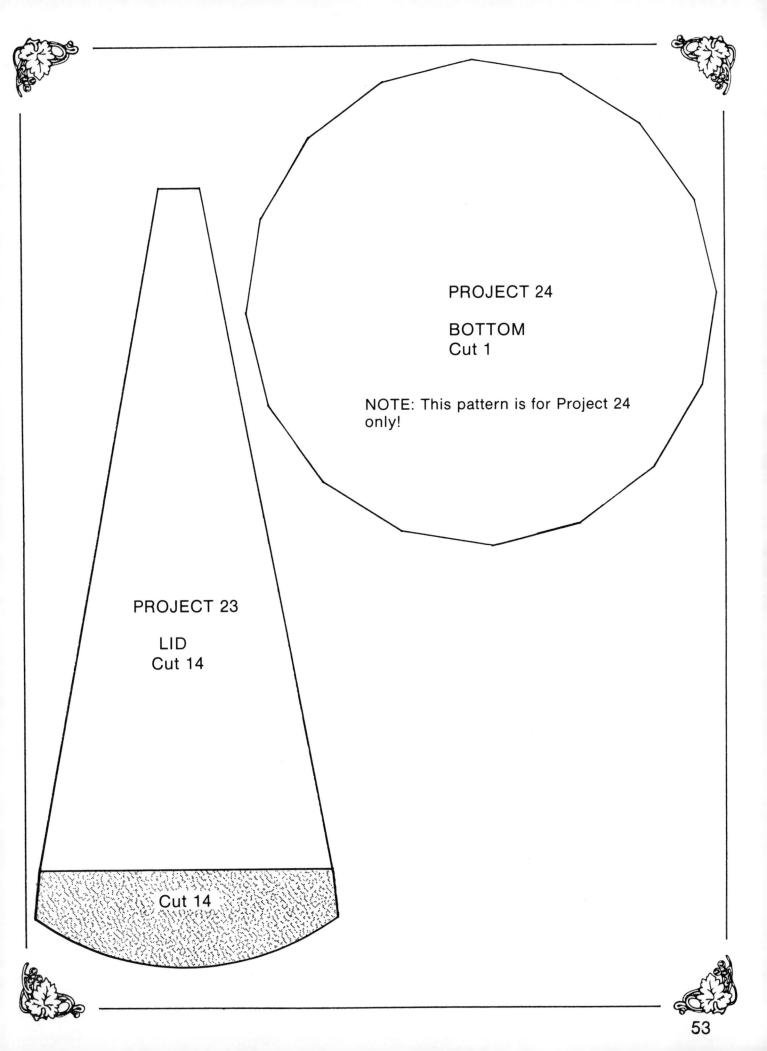

PROJECT 24

BOTTOM
Cut 1

NOTE: This pattern is for Project 24
only!

PROJECT 23

LID
Cut 14

Cut 14

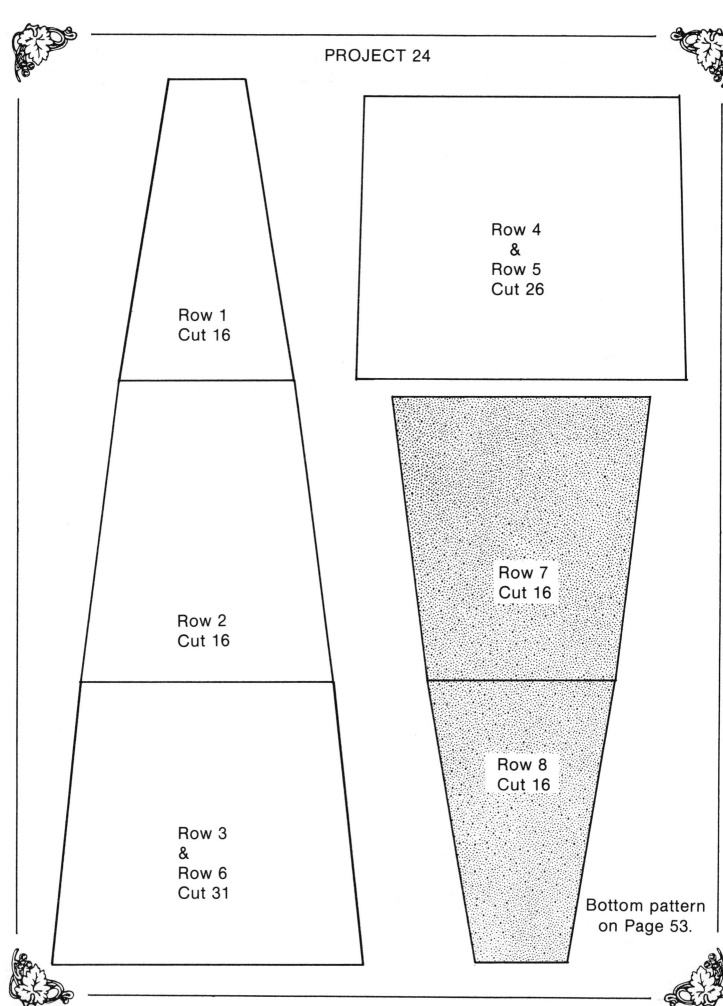

Row 1
Cut 16

Row 4
&
Row 5
Cut 26

Row 7
Cut 16

Row 2
Cut 16

Row 8
Cut 16

Row 3
&
Row 6
Cut 31

Bottom pattern
on Page 53.

# Bel-Air Gazebo

**SKILL LEVEL-** Int./Adv.    **Project 25**

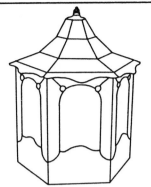

## SPECIFICATIONS

| | |
|---|---|
| # Pieces— | 61 |
| Height— | 14½" |
| Diameter— | 11½" |

Project Patterns on pages
55, 56 & 57.

## MATERIALS

— 1 sq. ft.— Lt. Blue Opal

— 1½ sq. ft.— Med. Blue Glue Chip

— 1¼ sq. ft.— Med. Blue Opal

— 1¾ sq. ft.— Lt. Blue Cath.

Vase Cap— 1¾"

Jewels— 12- 15mm (9/16") Blue

**Special Instruction—**
Eave overhang is added after the Lid has been attached to planter.

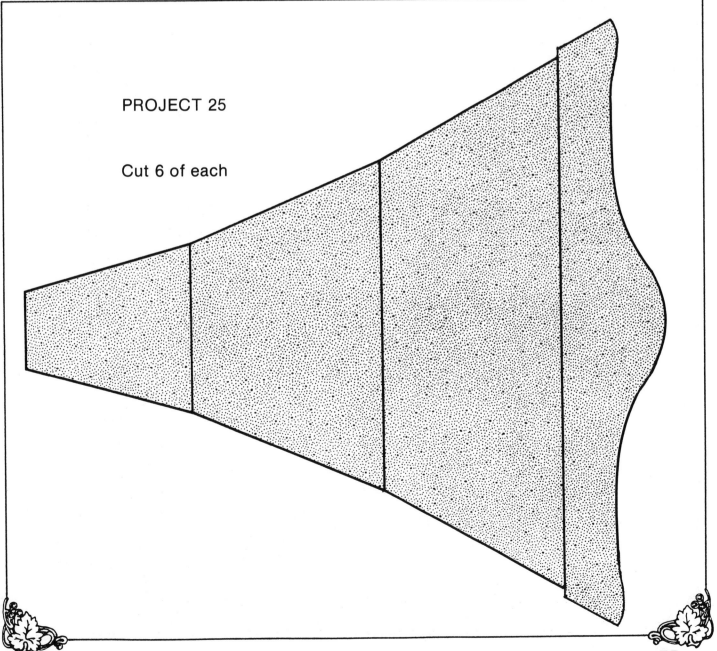

PROJECT 25

Cut 6 of each

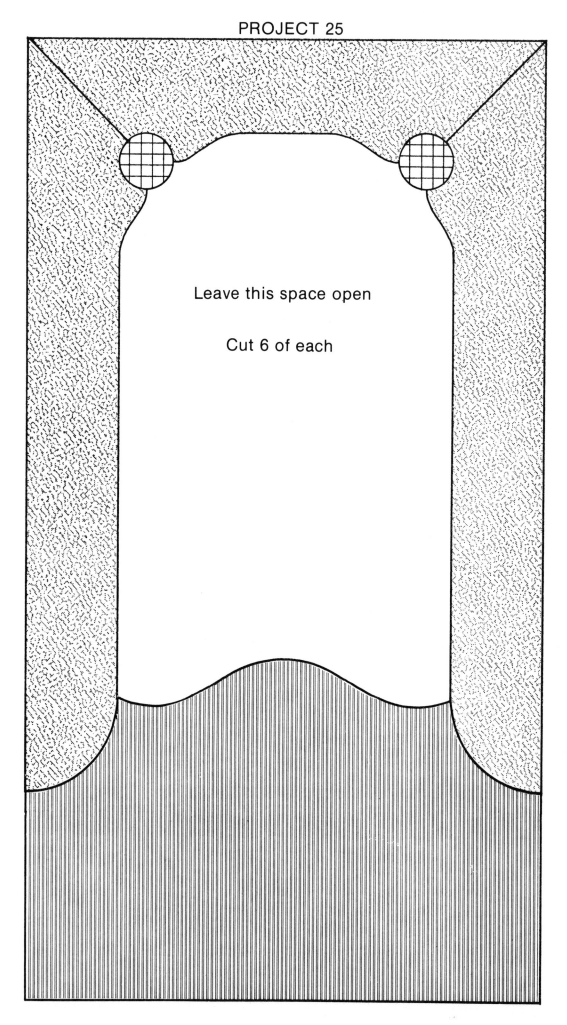

Leave this space open

Cut 6 of each

PROJECT 25

Bottom

Trace 2 halves to make one
complete pattern

Cut 1

## Teddy Bear

**SKILL LEVEL-** Beg./Int.  **Project 26**

### SPECIFICATIONS

| | |
|---|---|
| # Pieces— | 36 |
| Height— | 7½" |
| Diameter— | 6½" |

Project Patterns on page 59.
Fits a 6" Flower Pot

### MATERIALS

- — 2¼ sq. ft.— Beige Opal
- — 1/3 sq. ft.— Brown Opal
- — sm. piece— Beige Opal
- — sm. piece— Med. Yellow Opal
- — sm. piece— Dk. Yellow Opal

Nuggets— 6- amber

### Special Instruction—

For bottom cut a 5½" square . Glue doll eyes on for bear eyes. Bear nose is a glass overlay with a glued solder nose & wire mouth. Nuggets are overlays.

## Morning Glory

**SKILL LEVEL-** Beg./Int.  **Project 27**

### SPECIFICATIONS

| | |
|---|---|
| # Pieces— | 37 |
| Height— | 7" |
| Diameter— | 8" |

Project Patterns on page 60.
Fits a 6" Flower Pot

### MATERIALS

- — 2 sq. ft.— Iridescent White Opal
- — 1/8 sq. ft.— Blue/Purple Opal
- — 1/3 sq. ft.— Blue Opal
- — 1/8 sq. ft.— Dk. Green Opal
- — 1/8 sq. ft.— Med. Green Opal
- - sm. piece— Yellow Opal

### Special Instruction—

For bottom, cut a 4½" square.

## Bill's Planter Mobile

**SKILL LEVEL-** Beginner  **Project 28**

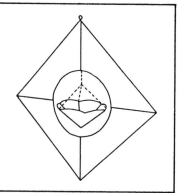

### SPECIFICATIONS

| | |
|---|---|
| # Pieces— | 10 |
| Size— | 12" x 12" square |

Project Patterns on page 61.

### MATERIALS

- — 12"x 12" sq. ft.— Aqua Blue Cath.

3—5" lengths jewel box chain.

### Special Instruction—

See instruction on pattern, page 61.

Pedestal (Optional)

Cut 4

Cut 1- Teddy Bear Panel
Cut 3- Plain Panels

BOTTOM- Cut a 5½" square.

Cut 1- Flower Panel
Cut 3- Plain Panels (use dotted line)

BOTTOM- 4½" X 4½" square- Cut 1

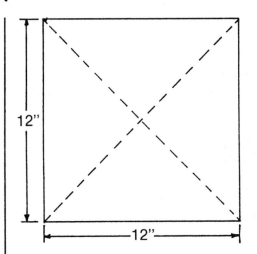
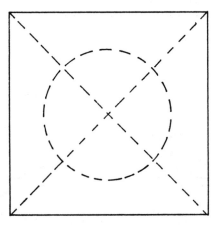
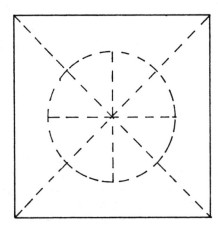

1. Draw the lines on your glass as shown in series of sketches and cut out.

2. Foil and solder the four outside frame pieces together.

3. Use *ONLY 6* of the pie shape pieces and construct the pot.

4. Solder 3 wires to the planter and a hook to the top inside of circle on frame.

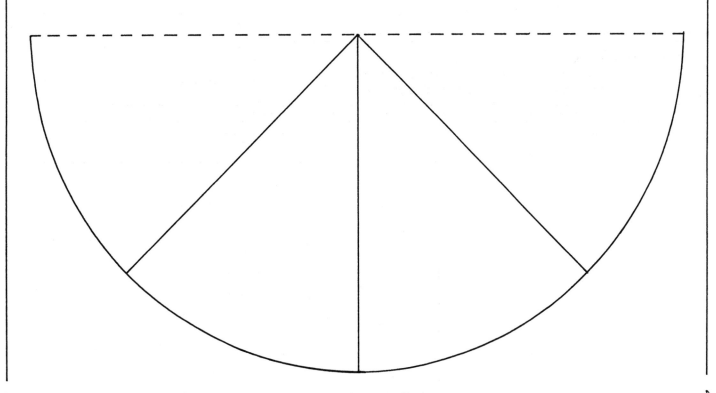

Trace two patterns to make one circle pattern piece.

| Brasila | SKILL LEVEL— Int. | Project 29 |

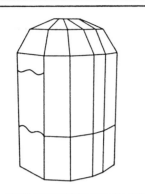

## SPECIFICATIONS

| # Pieces— | 50 |
| Height— | 15½" |
| Length- | 10" |
| Width— | 10" |

Project Patterns on pages 62, 63 & 64

## MATERIALS

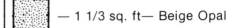

— 3¼ sq. ft.— Clear

— 1 1/3 sq. ft— Beige Opal

— ¾ sq. ft.— Lt. Amber Cath.

**Special Instruction—**
Build the dome top first and fit the planter to it, put the bottom on last.

---

| Crystal Palace | SKILL LEVEL— Adv. | Project 30 |

## SPECIFICATIONS

| # Pieces— | 154 |
| Overall Length— | 23"x 16" |
| Height— | Centre- 13" |
| | Ends- 9" |

Project Patterns on pages 65, 66 & 67

## MATERIALS

— 10 sq. ft.— Clear

— 1 1/3 sq. ft— Grey Opal

— 1/3 sq. ft.— Dk. Blue Cath.

— sm. piece— Lt. Blue Cath.

— sm. piece— Dk. Gr. Cath.

— sm. piece— Red Cath.

Jewels— 2- 24mm  (9/16") Red

**Special Instruction—**
Cutting must be accurate! The many angles will not assemble if the pieces fit poorly. Use a rod and tube hinge assembly for doors.

---

## PROJECT 29

TOP
Cut 1

BASE
Cut 8

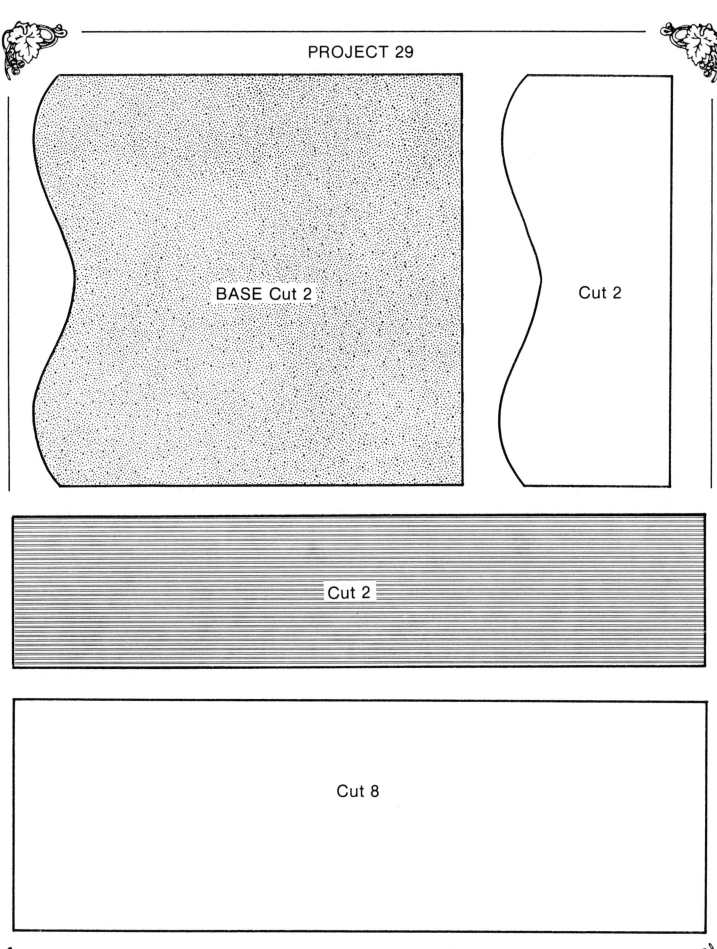

BASE Cut 2

Cut 2

Cut 2

Cut 8

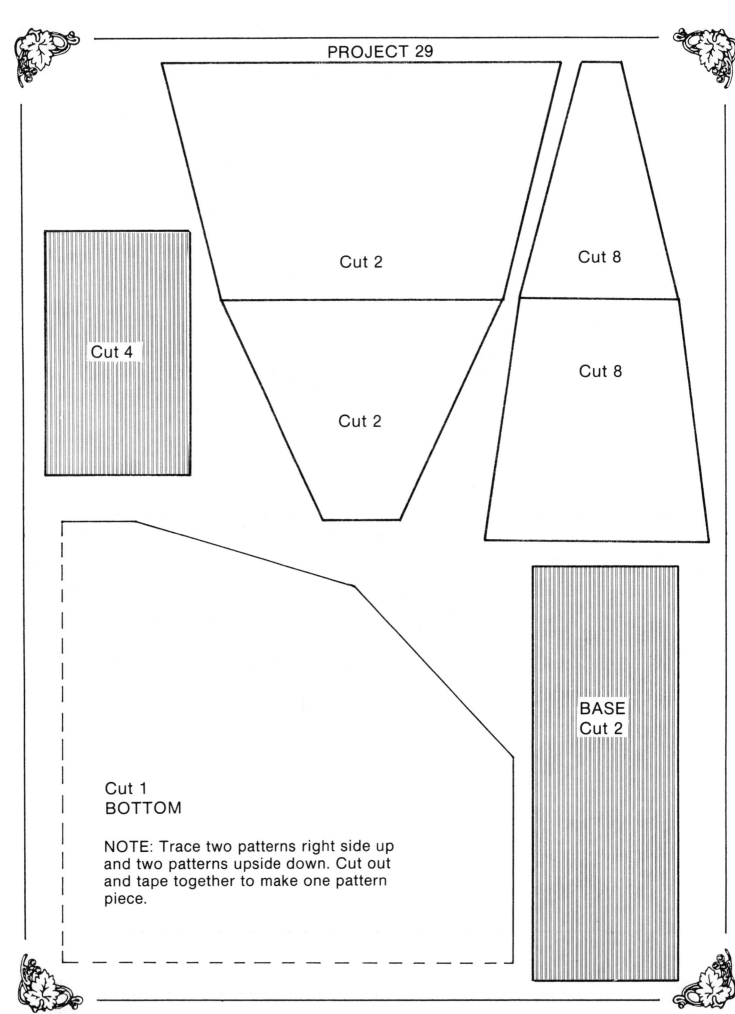

PROJECT 29

Cut 2

Cut 8

Cut 4

Cut 2

Cut 8

Cut 1
BOTTOM

NOTE: Trace two patterns right side up
and two patterns upside down. Cut out
and tape together to make one pattern
piece.

BASE
Cut 2

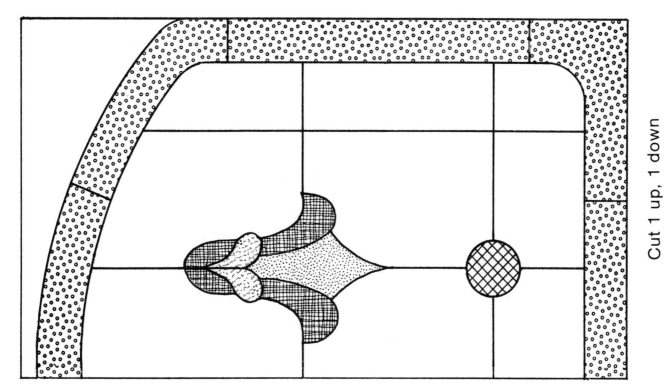

Cut 1 up, 1 down

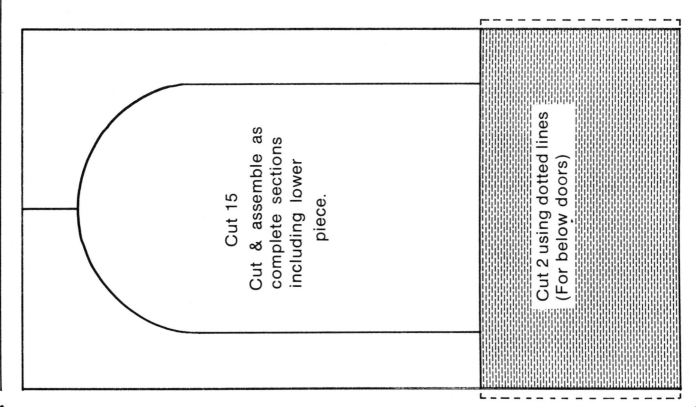

Cut 15
Cut & assemble as
complete sections
including lower
piece.

Cut 2 using dotted lines
(For below doors)

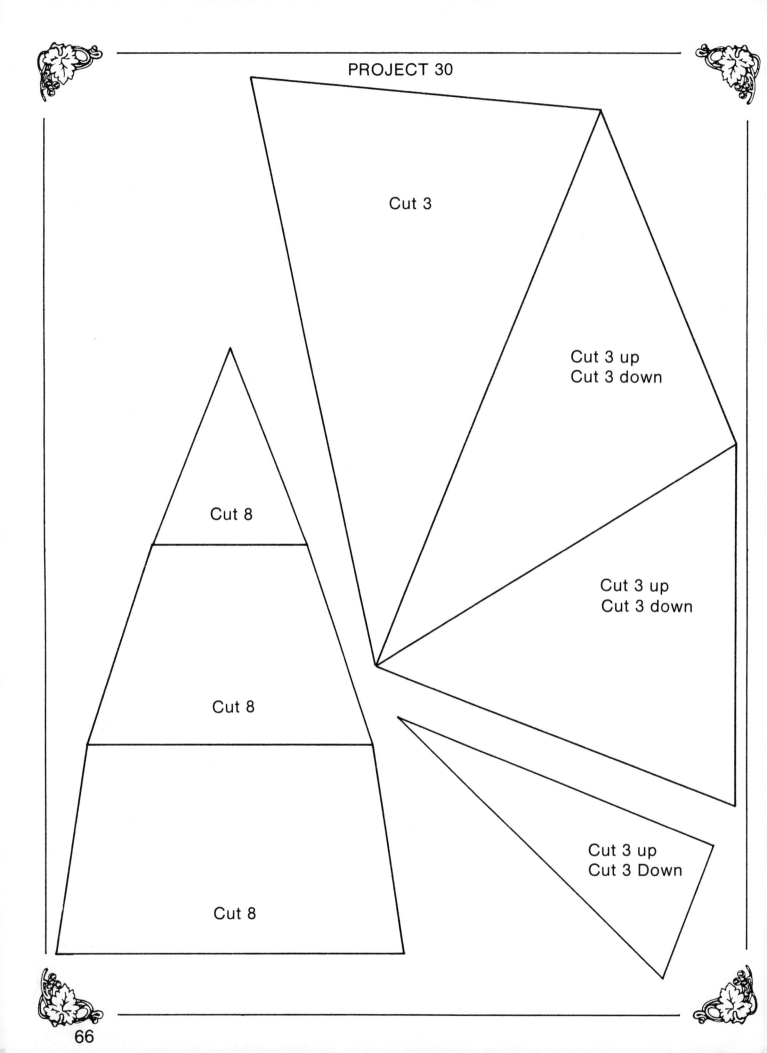

Cut 3

Cut 3 up
Cut 3 down

Cut 3 up
Cut 3 down

Cut 3 up
Cut 3 Down

Cut 8

Cut 8

Cut 8